DIOGENES

A quarterly publication of
THE INTERNATIONAL COUNCIL
FOR PHILOSOPHY AND HUMANISTIC STUDIES

INTERNATIONAL SCIENTIFIC COMMITTEE

President: T. Schabert (Erlangen University)

Y. Coppens (Collège de France), J. Labastida Martin Del Campo (National Autonomous University of Mexico), A. Laroui (University of Rabat), D. Pelletier (University of Lyon II), S. Rosen (Boston University), A. Schimmel (Harvard University/Bonn University), J. Starobinski (University of Geneva), R. Thapar (Jawaharlal Nehru University, New Delhi), S. Ueda (Kyoto University)

Berghahn Books
Providence • Oxford

DIOGENES

Director: **Jean d'Ormesson**
Editor: **Paola Costa**

The English language edition of *Diogenes* is published and distributed by
Berghahn Books
165 Taber Avenue, Providence, RI 02906-3329, USA
Tel: (401) 861-9330   Fax (401) 521-0046
E-mail: BerghahnBk@aol.com

Bush House, Merewood Avenue, Oxford OX3 8EF, UK
Tel: (01865) 742 224   Fax (01865) 744 978
E-mail: BerghahnUK@cityscape.co.uk

to whom all requests concerning subscriptions and information should be addressed. Editorial matters will continue to be handled by the Editor's office in France (*Diogène* – CIPSH, Unesco House, 1 rue Miollis, 75015 Paris).

Each annual volume is published in four issues, including index.
Annual Subscriptions
To order, by mail: Please send your request to *Berghahn Books* at the above address.

Parallel editions published simultaneously:
Arabic edition: National Centre for Unesco Publications, 1 Talaat Harb Street, Tahrir Square, Cairo, Egypt;
French Edition: Gallimard, 5 rue Sébastien Bottin, 75007 Paris;
Spanish edition: Universidad Nacional Autónoma de México, 3er circuito de la Investigación en Humanidades, Dr. Mario de la Cueva, Zona cultural, C.U., c.p. 04510, Mexico, D.F.

The articles published in *Diogenes* express freely the most diverse opinions, for which neither the Editors nor the Publishers can in any way be held responsible.

The journal is not responsible for manuscripts sent to the Editorial Office, nor can it return them unless they are accompanied by International Reply Coupons. Manuscripts are held for one year in the Editorial Office at the disposal of their authors.

© Copyright *Diogène*, 1996

Western Newspaper Publishing Co., Indianapolis

ISSN: 0392-1921

ISBN: 978-1-57181-121-9

DIOGENES
Number 174

Contents

The Link with Nature and Divine Mediations in Asia

Bernard Formoso An Ecological Theme	1
State Societies	
Gisèle Krauskopff Nepalese Chiefs and Gods	3
Marie Lecomte-Tilouine The Cult of the Earth Goddess among the Magar of Nepal	27
Bénédictine Brac de la Perrière The Burmese *Nats:* Between Sovereignty and Autochthony	45
Bernard Formoso Tai Cosmology and the Influence of Buddhism	61
Laurence Caillet Ties of Blood and Earth in Japan	83
Stateless Societies	
Pascal Bouchery The Relationship between Society and Nature among the Hani People of China	99
Gábor Vargyas Ancestors and the Forest among the Brou of Vietnam	117

* * *

Michel Jeanneret Portrait of the Humanist as Proteus	129
Gerhard van der Linde Shaped in the Image of Reason: The World According to Sherlock	155

* * *

Notes on the Contributors	167

An Ecological Theme

Bernard Formoso

Which traveler, passing through the rural communities of Asia, has not been intrigued by the existence, on the periphery of the village, of shrines, piles of stones, trees, or caverns ornamented with offerings which, at certain key moments during the year, become the focal points of an intense religious activity? These sites are in fact consecrated to chthonian forces that, next to the ancestors, occupy a high rank in the relationship that the peasants of Asia or other regions around the world establish with the divine. To be sure, the earth gods and the ancestors do not put themselves at the top of the pantheon that each society neatly builds for itself; but they nevertheless dominate the immediate sphere of individuals and social groups. They are at the center of their most routine cultic activities, and they are bestowed with a crucial role in the perpetuation of the groups with which they are identified and whose unity they symbolize.

On the one hand, the ancestors are charged with improving the fecundity, prosperity, morality, and cohesion of their descendants. The role of the earth gods, on the other hand, is to secure the livelihood of humans by ordering their connections with the natural environment. Since the former operate within a social group that is regulated by the rules of kinship, and since the objective of their activities is to assure the continuity of the descent group, the sphere of the earth gods in turn is not genealogical, but ecological, in the sense that it allows the local anchoring of a group of families that are not necessarily related. Beyond this, there exist many overlaps between the two categories: in some lineage societies, the ancestors of the founders of the village have been merged with the earth gods, whereas in other groups that are guided by a cognatic system, the communal spirits are in line with the principle of fictive kinship termed "grand-father and grand-mother" of the village.

The articles in this issue, which are part of a collective effort to be published in the near future, illustrate these propositions. At the same time they make it possible to differentiate, within the specific context of Asian societies, between two modes of representing the earth gods and the relationship with nature in which one corresponds to state societies and the other to tribal ones. In fact, the elaborate transformation of the environment that characterizes the state societies as they create wetland rice cultures or other permanently cultivated fields goes hand in hand with the transformation of the earth gods in a process of submission or ancestralization that is enshrined in the mythology; the humans seek to shape them in their own image, just as they try to model and tame the land in which they represent the active element. This ecological practice and the corresponding religious ideas contrast sharply with those of tribes that subsist in an itinerant agriculture of slash and burn or of stock-breeding, to the extent that the latter seek the patronage of the forces of nature by means of a contractual relationship without feeling the power to subvert them. This way of looking at things corresponds to a more direct and reversible harnessing of the environment.

The dividing lines between these two models may partly be undermined by the integration of tribal societies into a state structure which develops from the royal hold over the land and the entities that focus their energies. This is true of Burma since the eleventh century, or equally true of Nepal since the accession of the Shah dynasty at the end of the eighteenth century. The representations and forms of cult that relate to the earth gods reveal the existence of political links between the local and the central powers just as much as they reflect the ecological praxis of the societies under consideration. But in the final analysis and beyond these particular aspects, the earth gods as mediators invite us to consider the manner in which the agrarian societies of Asia or elsewhere reconcile questions of identity, ecological necessities, technical-economic means, political constraints, and religious beliefs within a comprehensive framework of their rapport with the world.

Nepalese Chiefs and Gods

Gisèle Krauskopff

Sacred Village Rocks and Groves

What Nepalese village or plot of land does not have a sacred tree or grove? The altar devoted to the earth gods is often the only collective shrine in a locality. Usually it is a natural site on the outskirts of the village, combining rocks and trees, and sometimes wooden shapes instead of rocks. It can also be associated with a cavity or hole in the earth. Thus among the Tamang of West Nepal: "The site of worship, which is known by the Nepalese term *bhumithan*, is located on a sharp incline overhanging the village; it is set up in a small sheltered area in the rock and divided into two areas by a raised flat stone."[1] Furthermore, we might add B. Pignède's description of the sanctuary as one finds it among the Gurung on the southern side of the Annapurna: "Three walls of rock hold up a little roof of flagstones, the facade being open to the outside. The wall at the back is cut by a large tree that covers the whole area with its shade, with the tree and rock forming a single mass ... Three raised rocks, the top of which is crudely rounded, are placed on a kind of tier. In the left corner is a little stone statue of a four-footed animal ... Finally, on the outside, in front of the sanctuary's open facade, a wooden post is set up ... The ensemble of the sanctuary includes a mixture of Indo-Nepalese and local elements."[2]

Likewise in central Nepal, in the nearby Magar country, J. Kawakita[3] notes that the different shrines devoted to Bhume are always situated under large trees. Elsewhere, the village sanctuaries sometimes look different. Among the Tharu in the Dang valley, for example, in the plain bordering southern Nepal, the village divinities are worshipped in several sites in which rocks are placed alongside effigies or wooden posts. A board shaped vaguely like a human marks the space devoted to the most important of them, the goddess Daharcandi, who controls all the dark powers prowling through the village terrritory, with large wooden nails and rocks at her side. The sanctuary of the earth gods, known as *bhuiyar*, is often no more than a mound of earth. In the western Dang, a single village sanctuary contains all the divinities of the place, and the *bhuiyar* gods are specifically represented by clay animal figurines erected in a hut on piles, whose northern post is devoted to the village chief.[4] This geography of the earth gods of the Tharu villages of Dang thus offers an interesting configuration, since here one finds, clearly distinguished from each other, the local goddess, a well-known figure from the popular Hindu religion and the local gods linked to the chief's district.[5]

These sacred sites combining earth, rock, and tree have certain ties to the sanctuary of the Chinese earth god. In fact, according to E. Chavannes,[6] the Chinese sanctuary requires a mound of earth and a tree, originally a sacred wood, thereby concentrating "all the creative and nurturing virtues of the earth." Later, the tree became a simple "signal," with the earth god being represented by a stone tablet, according to the idea, expressed by the famous Sinologist, that "rock is the hardest element in the domain of things dominated by the earth." With their standing rocks, some Nepalese altars likewise recall the megalithic sanctuaries of the tribal populations of central and northeast India. Thus, in each Nepalese locality, the sites welcoming the earth gods resemble one another: each is a "god-site" in which rocks and trees link the forces of the underworld to the heavens through archetypal natural supports, whose omnipresence in the Asia of the monsoons may be interpreted an indication of an ancient "earth cult."

Many-faced Deities

What deities are we talking about? Can they be defined, situated in the protean pantheon of Nepal? A recent anthology has demonstrated how vain it is to attempt to classify the gods of Southern Asia,[7] not only because they change identity and essential characteristics according to the context, but especially because ritual plays a key role in the shaping of their growing number. Thus among the Tharu of Dang, with the exception of rare heroical figures, the divinity is not really pinpointed, named, and imagined until the moment of the sacrificial act. Furthermore, as soon as one approaches a local divinity, the variability of forms and identities must be taken for granted.

There is, however, a general Nepalese term, *bhume* (from *bhui*, or "soil," "earth") that tends to unify all these powers linked to the earth. *Bhume, Bhumi,* and similar forms (*bhuiyar, bhanar, bhagar, bhumiya...*) are used throughout Nepal and in the southern borders of the Himilaya as well as in Northern and Central India. Among the Kirant populations, the least Hinduized of eastern Nepal, *bhume* accompanies the vernacular Tibetan/Burmese terms often restricted to a single ritual vocabulary – such as *bayaHap* among the Thulung Rai – or where the meaning differs, such as *ca:ri*, "the power of the territory," among the Mewahang Rai. Among the Tamang or the Gurung of central Nepal, influenced by Tibetan Buddhism, *bhume* sits alongside terms of Tibetan origin (*syibda ne:da* or *syihbda* in Tamang; *sildo nado* in Gurung, derived from Tibetan *gzih bdag gnas bdag* or *sa bdag*, "master of the earth").

The general usage of the term *bhume* in the hills and plains of Nepal is an interesting phenomenon. With the originally Tibetan denominative, it in fact spread in such a way that very few equivalent vernacular terms coexist, or else they refer, as among the Mewahang Rai, to different concepts. In the case of the Magar described by Kawakita, Bhume brings together, by a "Hindu baptism," gods of troubling variability and elasticity, whose only point in common is that they are linked to sites of "power." In so doing, he includes them in a geography that stretches beyond the boundaries of the village, all the while modifying their nature.

Bhume is not ruler of all the earth: he has friends, such as Bhairav, Ksetrapal, or even Mahadev-Shiva, who rule, often in a more violent fashion, over the telluric forces of the underworld.[8] Designating the earth, Bhume thus encompasses an idea both larger and more imprecise than the soil, but the god of the cultivated area that interests us here cannot, in most cases, be confused with an earth goddess. Hence the Tharu make a clear distinction between the earth, *dharti*, and the village gods of the soil, *bhuiyar*.

While the former comes from a quasi-metaphysical notion or a principle of respect and does not involve sacrifices, the latter are specific entities, tied to a definite place, who represent local authority and are worshipped in a village sanctuary of the same name. In short, a certain haziness maintains a balance that situates these gods somewhere between the tutelary divinities of the locality on the one hand, and the gods of the earth, conceived of as a mastered, inhabited, and exploited place, producing alimentary wealth, a place that has at times become the terrain of a political tutelage, on the other.

The minorities that live on the southern outskirts of the Himalayas, in the hills and in the deep valleys of the Terai, experienced the Hindu and Buddhist influences differently. Over the course of the last few centuries, the Indo-Nepalese, bearers of a more or less orthodox Hindu tradition, settled in the country to the west and east. With the unification of modern Nepal by a Hindu prince from the little principality of Gorkha at the end of the eighteenth century, this domination was solidly established both politically and socially. More diffused and less known were, on the other hand, northern Tibetan influence in the form of Lamaist Buddhism and that of the small states and chiefdoms influenced by this faith.

In villages with a majority of Indo-Nepalese population settled at a late date, there may still be natural sites, such as water holes, sources or cavities peopled by various divine forces, often a local goddess recalling popular Hindu tradition, but generally one does not find a collective *bhumethan* sanctuary. Elsewhere, in central Nepal, where Magar and Indo-Nepalese have long intermingled, the latter worship Bhume on a village level, paying tribute, in ambiguous fashion, to a Magar founding god.[9] More often, in fact, the Indo-Nepalese propitiate Bhume individually as a simple protective deity of the fields. We should note that in the Hindu milieu of the high castes, allegiances usually manifest themselves outside the village community, and the relationship between the territory and the earth appears to be different.

In the completely Tibetanized cultural regions of northern Nepal, the village sanctuaries are devoted to the traditional Tibetan god of the land, Yul Lha, who sometimes contains an aspect of the more ancient earth spirit (*sa bdag*), subjugated and transformed by a master of the Buddhist faith. The foundation of Lubra, a village practicing the Bon religion in the Tibetanized elevated valley of Mustang, is thus attributed to Trashi Gyaltsen, who subjugated two demons. These demons entrusted him with the earth upon which the village was built, then reappeared in the shape of poisonous snakes whom the Trashi Gyaltsen mastered and made his servants.[10]

Although similar to the gods of the soil of other communities heavily influenced by Tibetan Buddhism, such as the Tamang or the Gurung, the gods of Lubra present a different configuration. They have only survived as transformed, now demonic figures subjugated and absorbed by a more important god of the land. Even if they are named during certain rites involving the community, they do not have a place of worship of their own, giving way in the village to the temple marking the triumph of the Buddhist master and his faith. In the Tamang or Gurung regions, on the other hand, the "master of the soil" retains a central position in the collective cults of fertility and the protection of the village soil. It appears that it is in the villages in which the first inhabitants were tribal minorities that the sanctuaries of a god of the soil play an important role. However, we must not conclude that this god-site, paradoxically endowed with a Hindu name, is the last vestige of a past age, merely given a new name. The configurations are more complex. Thus, in the east of Nepal, in the Kirant country colonized at a late date by the Indo-Nepalese, and among the populations in which the Buddhist influence is almost non-existent, the village sanctuaries of the *bhumethan* type either do not exist or are much less important than in central Nepal. One finds, on the other hand, sacred sites with raised stones, associated with the territory of one of the founding clans (proto-clans).

Hence the cult of Bhume today instils the forces of the land into different socio-political areas. At one end of the spectrum, among the Hindus of the high castes, Bhume is a protective earth goddess in the most general sense, while the soil as a tutelary or social space is not part of this connotation. At the other end, as among the Kirant, he appears in sketchy form alongside concepts linked to the territories of proto-clans or ancestors, and one can still sense his different nature. Between the two poles, various configurations seem to overlap and even to reinforce each other, especially in those areas where the village appears as a quite well-defined social and spatial unit. This is the case among the Tharu or the Hinduized Magar of the west of the country or, in a different fashion, among the Tamang and the Gurung influenced doubly by Buddhism and Hinduism. As I shall attempt to demonstrate, the vast process of registering the country's land has contributed to the creation of this Nepalese Bhume with many faces. Linked to this process is the genesis of the village as a unit bound by social and political ties and land use, a unit more or less significant according to the region and the history of the land.

Earth-God Cults, Agrarian and Forest Rites

The existing descriptions of the cults of the earth gods emphasize the prosperity and the fecundity they bring to the outskirts of the village community. I would like to examine another aspect of these cults, namely how this prosperity finds its source in the forest areas around the village.

In the village of Dangsing in the Gurung country, a particular priest, the *khlibri*, celebrates the cult of the god of the soil five times a year in order to protect the village.[11] The ritual punctuates the calendar of agricultural activities, but it is particularly practiced in the months of June and July, just before the coming of the monsoon rains. It entails a ritual pheasant hunt. This hunt, which can last many days, is favorable to the coming of the rains and the pheasant obtained by this means is sacrificed along with a fish, the latter characterizing other offerings as well.

In the Tharu country, and more precisely among the Dang, two annual rites take place in the village sanctuary. The first during the dry season, is tied to the fallow lands, to the fear of fire and the mastering of the spirits of the dead who threaten the health of both man and livestock. As for the second, which corresponds to the sowing of the rice in August, it is meant to ensure the protection of the rice plants and involves the powers linked to the forest and to water. These forest forces are incarnated in wild beasts (the bamboo rat and the tiger), while those of the water take the shape of snakes (*nag*) and frogs. Although the custom has declined today, the men must leave for the forest in order to hunt the bamboo rat, which is alsolutely necessary to the sacrifice. The villagers insist upon the difficulty of the undertaking, for it takes several days to close in on the animal. During the ritual, which takes place during the night, the priest mediating the relation with the soil conceals himself beneath a cloth and buries side by side, behind the main effigies of the sanctuary, the body of the rat and an egg, symbol of the fecundity of the "tiger that suckles." As in the Gurung country, the forces of the forest and the water are closely tied to the prosperity of the fields. Elsewhere, the Tharu ritual in August, the more spectacular of the two, marks a strong time of the year; people recite the song of the origins of agriculture, the drums are "opened," and their benediction sets off the cycle of dances. Finally, a possessed person dances on fire. This annual ritual is the repetition, on a smaller scale, of the ritual of village claustration enacted for the founding or symbolical refounding of a village, during which the forest resumes possession of the inhabited site.

This configuration, which links the prosperity of the village to the surrounding forests and associates the ritual hunt with agrarian cycle, is still more obvious in certain tribal communities in north-eastern India. Thus, among the Bondo of Orissa, the veneration of the earth goddess in the rock sanctuary of the village sets off, in April, two weeks of ritual hunting that correspond to the setting on fire of the fallow lands and has as its goal, as do the other regular village rites, the favoring of the fecundity of the earth. In this context, the success or failure of the hunt indicates the quality of the harvest.[12] On the day of the offering to the earth goddess, the principal officiant is cloistered in the village, and all the villagers must camp out in the forest.

In the rites devoted to the Nepalese land gods, this opening of the village to the powers of the surrounding land is only rarely expressed in the form of a ritual hunt or village cloistering. Nonetheless other information confirms the close and rather general link between Bhume and untamed forces, aquatic as well as sylvan. Bhume is often split into Syame Bhume or Sime Bhume, the first term designating muddy or damp earth. Hence, among the Magar of the North, who speak the Kham language, every year in February and March, during the first ritualized passing of the swing-plough, the rite of *halsar* is addressed to the earth god Bhume. This god is then evoked in the form of a snake, which the astrologer officiant brings to the center of the designated field. The ritual inaugurates the agricultural season and "opens" the fields.[13] But it is also to Sime Bhume ("god of dry and humid earth") that the hunters address themselves in order to obtain success, and he is given part of the entrails of the hunted animal (in the company of the spirits of the hunter, the forest, the dead, and the god of the summits, Braha). Lastly, a final sacrifice exclusively to Sime Bhume closes the hunting season. A similar association between Bhume, Sime, the snake divinities and forest divinities (more exactly of the hunt, like Sikari) is found among the southern Magar of the Gulmi district who speak Nepalese. According to M. Lecomte-Tilouine, who emphasizes the essentially forest nature of Bhume,[14] at the time of the cult of Bhume the custom is to release a chicken into the forest. Among the Tamang of the West, the god of the soil is also worshipped during the rituals propitious to the success of a hunt. Hunting and farming are both part of the same cycle of exchange between the untamed world and village life.

Of course, in his Nepalese identity as Bhume, the god of the soil is first and foremost an owner and protector of cultivated lands. In the Hindu milieu of the high castes, as – it would appear – in the villages of northern and central India, his figure tends even to diminish to that of a beneficient divinity of fields cultivated by a domestic unit. However, this deity has a much more ambivalent character in Nepal, and for many writers, as we have seen, it is essentially linked to the untamed world. Certain rites even bring up a more extreme concept: a village must be opened up to the forest in order to assure prosperity, in some ways and at least symbolically, to deny its existence and return to the time of its origins. In the case of the Gurung or Tharu rituals presented above, the god of the soil transcends the opposition between the cultivated site and the forest. He is situated between two of its borders, regulating the relationship between the two worlds.

The god of the soil can then become an autochthonian god, imagined or real, referring back to the imagined time of a first foundation. By symbolically reinstating the time that preceded the genesis of a social group, the opening up of the village to the forest makes this mediating god the guarantor of the community he redefines. He is, furthermore, particularly pure, as is indicated by the isolation and sacralization of the officiants, of a single sanctuary or the whole village. In this respect, he holds power over the course of community life and is contacted in crucial moments of the calendar year in which the future of the community is concerned. The socio-political organization of the community is therefore at stake in his cult.

Earth Gods and Village Chiefs

The cult of the gods of the soil have customarily been treated as the expression of a more or less archaic religious tradition, an approach often linked to the question of the double category of priests. Alongside the shaman who works with unexpected disturbances, the "tribal priest" is in charge of the regular cults, such as those addressed to the earth god. In all the communities of Nepal where his function is certified, this priest in fact maintains a close relationship with the divinity. He assures him of worship, and this is in fact one of his main functions.[15] There are, however, villages in which there is no "tribal chief." To the west of Nepal, among the Magar, and among the Kham-speaking population of the North where the shaman infiltrates the entire religious field, as well as among people from the more Hinduized South, the "tribal priest" has been replaced by non-specialists as officiant of the cults of the soil, in particular the chief of the community or the eldest of the founding or dominant clan, who can be also be the chief. M. Lecomte-Tilouine has well demonstrated the political and social implications of the chief's role in the Magar cults of Bhume.[16]

When he is not the officiant of the rite, the chief is in any case concerned with a cult that affects the community as a whole. In most of the Nepalese communities, he is closely associated with the priest because he collects the funds necessary for the cult, or seconds the officiant, or, more notably, because he maintains certain ritual prerogatives as a descendant of the founding clan. Furthermore, in places where the duties differ, the "tribal priest" and the chief can be one and the same person, combining the leadership of the community and the communication with the earth god. This is, for example, the case among the Tamang, where the configuration varies significantly for our purposes. Thus A. Höfer notes that "the chief *mukhiya* ... is in charge of the cult of *syibda ne:da* through his function. The *mukhiya* is either a descendant of the first inhabitants of the village, or he belongs to the most important local clan segment ... In a more general fashion, as the person responsible for the cult, he is also called *lambu* ('tribal priest')."[17]

More concisely, according to B. Steinmann, among the Tamang of the East the duty of the "tribal priest" has not been certified; rather the village chief takes charge of these cults. He automatically has the title of religious mediator between humans and the divinities of the soil and earth. Duties as mediator and as chief seem here to be merge into the function of the *tamba*, a sort of bard, village chief, and master of ceremonies who is the counterpart of the "tribal priest" and chief among the Tamang of the West. As B. Steinmann notes, the guarantee of his religious power comes not from an initiation, but from an ancient contract between the divinities of the soil and man.[18]

It is therefore as representatives of the gods of the soil and mediators between these gods and the community that the chief and "tribal priest" are identified among the Tamang. Similar things are found in an entirely different context, among the Tharu in the valley on the Dang. There, the priests, through hereditary right, have the privilege to officiate over the fixed sanctuary (village or domestic) where the god of the soil rules, and they are distinguished from the non-hereditary officiants, "the masters of the forest," who deal with errant untamed forces. Among the hereditary priests, there are those who, on the one hand, "hold the country together" (*desbandhiya*) by taking charge of a "kingdom" made up of several villages, and, on the other hand, those who officiate on behalf of individual houses. In both cases, they are considered to be the descendants of gods who are both the ancestors of the priest clans and masters of their earth. The northernmost post of the hut that houses these gods is furthermore devoted to the village chief who, with his close ancestors, "the new gods of the soil," and the earth god, makes up the category of gods known as *bhuiyar*. The terminology and the spatial arrangement create a clear association among these three poles: the god of the soil, the master of a "kingdom," the earth priest and the chief. They confirm the major role of the link to the soil (either founded or acquired) in this configuration.

We should not be surprised to learn that the Tharu priest of the soil until recently belonged to the same clan as the chief of the region, when he wasn't the chief himself. These regional chiefs, or *caudhari*, were the delegates of the ancient Hindu king of Dang-Salyan, then the autocracy of the Rana ministers who controlled the central power from 1845 to 1951. The priests of the soil west of Dang are said to have received their ritual privilege directly from the king of Dang-Salyan, a vassal of the king of Nepal and his Rana ministers until 1961. This privilege was largely responsible for the political and economical prosperity of the clans that held juridical and ritual authority over the earth. This being the case, the pairing of chief and priest of the soil varies a great deal from east to west, and from north to south in the country of the Dangara Tharu, acording to local political contexts. The existence of the very centralized function of the priest of the soil, as well as that of the strong man as master of a region, was in this case engendered by the royal delegation of rights to the earth. It was also created, through force, by the modification of the ancient structures of local power, about which we unfortunately know practically nothing. In any case, these facts underline the importance that the delegation of the king's authority has over the land in the current forms of the cult of the earth god and the social units it governs.

A God of Land Registration

As soon as one speaks of the chief and political authority, the question of the area of authority immediately comes into play. Ethnography often leads one to imagine that the village, with its sanctuary and its chief, forms a well-defined unit whose worshipping of earth gods assures its permanence. While such an impression is justified for the Tharu of Dang or in the northern Tibetanized regions that we have left outside of purview of this study, the focusing on the village, especially in the middle country, ignores other, more significant units. M. Gaborieau has well demonstrated that in the hills of central and eastern Nepal, unlike in India, the notion of the village (*gau*) is misleading and reductive, especially when referring to the time before the administrative and political establishment of the village panchayats in 1962. On this subject he writes: "The word *gau* never applies to a single well-defined type of territorial unit only ... The smallest territorial unit in Nepal is the area of jurisdiction, the *taluk*, of a chief from the founding lineage recognized by the royal authority and called *talukdar* in the administrative nomenclatures, but known more often as *mukhiya*, *subba*, or *dware*, depending on the place and ethnic group. This basic unit can be more or less large – from a few houses to a few dozen houses – and its size varies according to administrative factors (form of land tenure) and especially to factors tied to the social structure of ethnic groups who exercise power there."[19]

I would like to emphasize in particular the different forms of land tenure and the role they play in the definition of the areas of authority of the local chiefs. Moreover, the approach based on land tenure allows us to avoid the dilemma of the following issues: are these territories or more specifically social groups? These units of land are in fact centered around a group of farmers, the earth being measured according to the wealth thus produced.

In particular, the different types of land tenure have involved various forms of the delegation of royal power. In fact, the administrative land registration and the political centralization that accompanies it did not take place all at once after the unification of Nepal by the dynasty of the Shah at the end of the eighteenth century. For not only do the political and social substrata vary according to ethnic milieu, as M. Gaborieau points out; they also vary because the west and central Nepal had already experienced an "initial centralization" of government power among the little Hindu principalities of which the westernmost date from the fourteenth century, at the latest. This cadastral registration, principally of land, influenced the genesis of "villages" and the status of their chiefs, now the intermediaries between the former local structures and the central government. The superimposition of central power over these little-understood political and territorial structures is at the heart of the transformations of the hypothetical ancient gods of the soil (and of power) into gods of the soil of a delegated chief, into gods of the type of Bhume henceforth celebrated on regular dates on the agrarian calendar. Added to this is the recent impact of the division into Panchayats, which we shall not go into here, but which not only radically modified the local representation of the chiefs elected thereafter, but redesigned a new village unit.[20]

The ethnographers working in the Kirant country, to the east of Nepal, thus noted the lack of importance of the concept of the village before the founding of the Panchayats. Among the Kulunge Rai, there is not one chief with authority over the whole village, but a series of chiefs, from each of the local clans. No one of them has real authority and means of coercion over the others. The number of these clan chiefs even multiplied after the populations of east Nepal were brought under the system of the Panchayats. In these regions, the habitat is dispersed and the "village" often stretches over the whole side of a mountain, although this use of space is not the only cause. In fact, in the Tamang countries further to the west, the habitat is just as dispersed, but the village seems to form a better defined geographic and ritual entity, marked by cults of gods of the soil.[21]

In the case of the Limbu of the Kirant country, the neighbors of the Rai to the west, the fragmentation of power and the non-existence of the village as a social and territorial unit must be considered in relation to the *kipat* land system peculiar to this region. As it was instituted after the conquest, this tenure represents a syncretism between local customs and the law of the Shah kings.[22] At the end of the eighteenth century, the Shah king of Gorka, the unifier of Nepal, allowed the Limbu kings, henceforth called *subba*, to manage their ancestral lands, on condition of paying a tax to the central government. This land system allowed for the maintenance of power over the soil of the ancient clan chiefs but also engendered a competition. This in turn caused the land prerogatives of the local chiefs to be divided up. These local units never became part of a village with set boundaries, or rather, "the village" of the 1960s found itself with several chiefs.

In other words, in the particular case of the Limbu, one notes that the cult of Bhume does not in fact seem to play a role on the village level. Ph. Sagant mentions the marginal propitiation of Bhume in the form of oaths, linked to the Gurkha domination, in which the earth is to some extent called as witness.[23] On the other hand, the original territory of the clan is always valorized and centered on a fortress associated with the god of the land, on the one hand, and on an ensemble of erected stones tied to the founding incest of the group. Once a year, these founders are evoked during the annual ritual of the divinity Mangenna, who is attached to the power of the ancient clan chiefs. If ever there was an earth god in the land of the Limbu, it would be Mangenna, the god of the territory of the original clan, and especially of Nahangma, who guarantees the power of the head of the household and "allows access to a parcel of the ancestors' land to the head of the household."

The absence of a structured village cult to Bhume should be linked to the maintenance of these earlier forms of power and ancient territorial and social units, in this case the clan territories, through the transitory land system of *kipat*. The Limbu are among the only minorities to have retained this relative autonomy, symbol, and support of their identity. The Indo-Nepalese migrants who settled in the region were, furthermore, under another land regime, the *raikar*, which is predominant in the hilly regions of Nepal. In this form of land tenure, the king is the nominal owner of the earth, which he gives directly to his subjects to farm, with the intermediaries responsible for the collection of land tax on the non-irrigated lands being the *talukdar* chiefs or *mukhiya* named to the administrative districts outlined by the central government. Thus the Rai, neighbors to the west of the Limbu, did not succeed in maintaining the same autonomy of land, since a large part of this region had been in *raikar* control from a more distant time. The agrarian cult of the village god Bhume has been verified there, though it has none of the political dimension found in the Tharu or Magar countries to the west of Nepal. Among the Thulung Rai this cult appears without great force, the "tribal priest" officiating to a very weak following.[24] Among the Kulung Rai, the agrarian rites seem to involve much vaster units than the "village," uniting all the heads of households and bringing the ancestors into play.[25]

We should note that behind the notion of prosperity attached to the Nepalese Bhume is sometimes found, such as among the Mewahang Rai of the valley of the Honku, the idea of *ca:ri*, of "territorial force" related to a cult devoted to the rocks of the ancestors of the proto-clans. According to M. Gaenzle, this force is controlled by the "knowledge" the legitimate proprietors of the territory acquire either through dreams or through the close link of communication that ownership of the soil and political power imply. The author furthermore notes that the cult has undergone an evolution linked to the disintegration of the political unit and the division of the posts of the local functionaries.[26] In other communities in the hilly regions of Nepal, one finds traces of comparable things obliterated by the existence of a single sanctuary to the village god Bhume. Thus among the Gurung, the term *to* designates both the territory "of the village" and its guardian deity, as well as "the lands of a certain number of houses," and "the quarter of a straggling village,"[27] suggesting a possible link with the territorial unit of a part of the clan. It would appear then that the Indo-Nepalese god Bhume only identifies a power within the framework of different types of delegations of the royal authority over the land, where the village and its chief have managed to expand, without opposing other types of local power, such as the heads of clans, segments of clans, or households.

Let us shift our focus to the center and west of Nepal, where centralized authority was imposed under different historical conditions and where *raikar* land tenure was implanted long ago. The weak sense of the notion of the village and the division of local power are also present there, to varying degrees depending on the region. According to M. Gaborieau, in the Tanahon district of central Nepal (peopled with Indo-Nepalese, Magar, and Gurung) many district chiefs (*taluk*), tied to ancient segments of founding clans, share the power in the same locality. However, the author emphasizes vaster units: the cantons, *thum*. These have at their head a "great chief," or *mahamukhiya*, in direct communication with the central power and to which the district chiefs or *mukhiya* are subordinate. These cantons are the result of an administrative parcelling of the land following the unification of Nepal and were in effect until 1962. M. Gaborieau stresses their political and ritual unity. Of particular interest to us is the fact that one of the cults that embodied this unity was the worship of Bhayar (alias Bhume), which took place in the canton's sole sanctuary. The "great chief" was responsible for the cult, independently of any directive from the centralized power, and all the heads of households were supposed to participate in this.[28] Such cantonal cults of Bhume have been noted in other regions near central Nepal.

The link between Bhume and the administrative and land registration appears clear in this case, since this cult is associated with a district defined by the central government and whose seat is no longer a clan territory. The "great chief's" authority over the soil is directly delegated by that of the king. Certainly, as a *mukhiya* chief himself, he can be the descendant of a segment of the founding clan, but the seat of his power, the canton, transcends these ancient divisions. Moreover, it appears that in matters concerning the legitimation of power, the Dasai festival, concretizing that of the Hindu sovereign, takes precedence. M. Gaborieau thus sees the cantonal ritual of Bhume as a cult of prosperity without political dimension, in contrast to the Dasai festival. The Dasai ritual also took place in the center of the *thum*, and it was the *mahamukiya* who executed it. Even if certain *mukhiya* chiefs are the descendants of the founding fathers, and in contrast to what happened under the *kipat* land system, they have to some extent lost their ancestral link to the soil; they became more the holders of an administrative function than the chosen masters of the soil god embodying the founding father. In the region studied by M. Gaborieau, in this respect it is very significant that the Gurung population, settled at the most ancient date, no longer has any *mukhiya* post.

We have yet to explore the origin of the division into cantons, which might help us better to understand the evolution of the structures of political power and the status of the god Bhume within this structuring. Indeed it is unlikely that these cantons were created out of nothing. As well-defined administrative and ritual units, they reflect a more ancient state of centralization in central Nepal. This region had in fact been under Hindu rule since the fifteenth century. Thus in the district of Gulmi located to the west of the district of Tanahon and peopled with equal numbers of Magar and Indo-Nepalese, the Gurka State reused the ancient local divisions into six small principalities for the new administrative divisions.[29]

In central Nepal, the cantonal cult of Bhume was thus henceforth part of a continuity, reflecting an earlier, more successful process of political centralization. In other words, a "first centralization" would have influenced the formation and composition of the territorial divisions into cantons and villages. To speak of a "first centralization" is to recall facts of which, unfortunately, there are few historical traces; the Hindu princes of central Nepal indeed supplanted the local chiefs, probably "Magar" or "Gurung," who are known today as the "old kings" of the "Magar country."[30] The question, however, remains as to the nature of the territorial units these pseudo-kings – most certainly clan chiefs rather than kings according to Hindu criteria – might have governed. It appears in any case that a certain territorial continuity was maintained. The present-day villages of the Gulmi region would date back to the time of the "old kings."

Thus the village of Argha, in Gulmi, is the center of a canton, but it is also a *kot*, an ancient royal fortress housing the tutelary goddess of the Hindu dynasty who reigned there before the unification of Nepal. This was the site where, each year, the power of the king was regenerated (in the person of the symbolic heir of the local dynasty) during the great festival of Dasai. As remarkable as it may seem, Bhume was also worshipped there. The association we noted earlier between Bhume and the Hindu goddess of power on the level of the cantonal cults of the district of Tanahon is taken even further here, indicating a more ancient and widespread process of centralization.

And what of other regions in which the delegation of power took place differently? Let us take the case of the Tharu from the Dang valley, a Terai valley that had been under the lordship of a Hindu king since at least the fourteenth century. The ecology is totally different from that of the hill country; a deadly marsh climate and the great quantity of forest limited the settling of the area until the 1950s. As early as the fourteenth century, the non-resident Brahmins and the Nath Yogi, close Shivaite ascetics closely identified with the royal power, received enormous donations of land there under two forms of tenure: the *birta*, profiting individuals usually of the Brahmin cast, and the *guthi*, endowments for the cult of a god, in this case the god of the Nath. As opposed to the *raikar*, these two types of land tenure have in common that the king completely transfers his rights to the beneficiaries. I cannot go into the complex story of the ancient Dang kingdom, pinched between the powers from the hills and those from the Gange plains, but after the conquest of part of the valley it remained a vassal kingdom of the Shah. In this system (*rajya*), which was abolished in 1961, the vassal profited directly from the taxes on the lands in his kingdom, just like the holders of *birta* and *guthi*. All these properties were very important: each domain was counted by "villages," the largest including more than a dozen. These three types of land tenure created veritable small states within a state in Dang.

Unlike what one finds in the *kipat* land regime, a strong centralization and a reinforcement of local powers developed. Each Tharu village in Dang formed, until recently, a compact unit or *mauja*, bringing together the households making use of a *birta*, *guthi*, or *rajya* land. Only a part of the harvest went to the Tharu peasants, and the land was managed by intermediaries, the village chiefs, the *mahaton*. These chiefs answered to the *caudhari*, who were in charge of a grouping of several villages called a "kingdom," and retained, as we have seen, a ritual authority over this same soil. These regional Tharu chiefs were the delegates of land holders who did not live in the domains. They controlled the distribution of the lands to the peasants, collected the taxes, managed the statute labor system, guaranteed local justice while profiting from a rise in fines and, after the institution of the Hindu code of the Rana in 1854, even regulated the appurtenance belonging to the Tharu "caste." They vouchsafed the prosperity of their "kingdom" and some even built fortresses. The regional sanctuaries of the *caudhari* chiefs have disappeared today, but a sign of this ancient system remains today in each village. The god of the soil, formerly the god of the region, is today worshipped strictly on the level of villages of the same *parganna*, under the auspices of the village chief and the regional priest, with the latter belonging imperatively to the main clan of the earth god in question. As opposed to the Limbu *subba*, the Tharu regional chiefs were veritable small kings, managing a vast amount of land. In particular, these land entities and the power of the great Tharu chiefs that upheld them was much more the product of the delegation of royal power than the survival, as in the Kirant or Magar countries, of ancient clan territories. It is in fact likely that at an ancient date the Tharu, quasi-nomadic clearers of marsh forests, did not form a territorial unit or stable clan. The centralized cult of the god of the soil is linked to the particular land tenure system that developed in the Dang valley and which engendered well-circumscribed territories, bringing together compact villages. Unlike those in the east and west of Nepal, the Tharu village is neither the territory of the founder nor a conglomerate of territories of segments of clans, but a unit exploiting a domain of land.

Other facts relative to the centralization of the cult of the god of the soil are found elsewhere and confirm the link between Bhume and the administrative and land registration of Nepal. In the Kirant country, among the Thulung Rai, N. J. Allen [31] has noted that the institution of the "tribal priest," which we saw to be closely associated with the cult of the god of the soil and the chiefdom, was originally tied to that of the small princes who governed before the conquest during the 1770s. He notes, moreover, that the village of Mukli, considered the first permanent Thulung village, has on its grounds the two most ancient sanctuaries of the god of the soil Bhume that appear to have retained pre-eminence, where the "tribal priest" officiates, though the rite is on the path to extinction and draws only small crowds. Furthermore, the founding myth of these sanctuaries and thus of the gods of the soil suggests a link between certain villages and an ancient political hegemony. These facts do not, however, allow us to say whether the areas in question were the territories of chiefs of clans, cantons, *thum*, or other princely divisions.

For the Tamang of the East, B. Steinmann[32] also traces a filiation between the ancient *talukdar*, responsible for the collection of taxes of an area within a canton, and the local chiefs today, masters of ceremony in charge of a village god of the soil. B. Pignède mentions the existence of regional sanctuaries tied to ancient structures of local power preexisting the imprint of the Hindu dynasty of the Shah, and later that of the Rana. For the Thulung Rai, was it a question of clan territories of the ancient Kirant clans, as it is among their Limbu or Mewahang neighbors? In this case, the cult of Bhume would have subsumed the cults of the ancient gods of the soil, in a completely different territorial and land-tenure structure. For the north in the Gurung and Tamang countries, what we encounter in the Ghale principalities is a "first centralization," strongly marked by a Tibetan influence and preceding the imprint of the Hindu Shah kings. In short, it is not impossible that the regional cults of Bhume are less ancient than certain authors suggest: in the Tharu area, the regional sanctuaries are clearly associated with a late date (eighteenth and nineteenth centuries) during which the chiefs of this group received orders from higher powers.

Be that as it may, all the examples we have cited emphasize a phenomenon of centralization: the cults to the village gods of the soil today derive from cults that took place on a much larger scale (canton, small principality or local chiefdom), thereby reflecting the administrative registration of a Nepal in the process of unification. All this took place during a period of transition, which saw the passing of units of local power of varying nature to districts governed by a chief who had received the delegation of an authority over the land from a king whose power and districts under his protection were subsequently modified. A chief who held complete power granted by the local gods were replaced by a master of principally land-related authority, delegated by the king of kings. In fact, even if certain *mahamukhiya* have retained limited judiciary prerogatives, or even, like the *subba* of the Kirant country, the right to maintain an army, the essentials of power of the local chiefs, particularly to the west and central Nepal, was reduced to the management of a domain of land of which they had been given charge.

The facts concerning the centralized nature of the function of the "tribal priest" go back, moreover, to the controversial question of the double category of priests. In the above-mentioned examples, the "tribal priests" seem to have considered their role reinforced around the poles of local power that formed at the time of the unification of Nepal. Did they consolidate their position even while the chiefs they served submitted themselves to an administrative power? Elsewhere, as among the most Hinduized and most anciently integrated Magar, for example, the chiefs, on the contrary, continued to interact directly with the god of the soil.

Political Power, Land Ownership, and the Gods of the Soil

If the cult of the village god of the soil Bhume has a political side, it expresses an overlordship enacted by the delegation of a single aspect of royal sovereignty: ownership of land. This delegation modified the relationship between the former chiefs and the soil or a territory and took on various forms depending on the systems of land tenure put into effect. These influenced the formation of the human "landscape," the composition of the "villages" or cantons, depending on the degree of development of the models of the Hindu sovereignty already in place.

Thus, in the Kirant country, one still sees the ancient territorial organization of the founding clans in part aborted by the implantation of the god Bhume: the existence of a "double power" bears witness to this situation. Conversely, among the Tharu to the west of Nepal, the chiefs forged their power by integrating a control that registered an originally "empty" land.[33] The god of the soil reigning at the center of the domains of land and the villages that composed them illustrate the result of this process. As for the Magar, they seem to have maintained a link to the land of their founding ancestors, but the land was re-registered according to the order of the first small Hindu kings with whom they closely collaborated. Bhume triumphed here as a village god, guarantor of its political and territorial unity although subjugated to a foreign power. But in the fortresses of the former principalities that were the poles of this "first centralization," and in the cantons that replaced them, Bhume lost all political aura, giving way to the Hindu warrior goddess.

This more or less successful administrative registration reflects a distinct regional history in which the east and west appear particularly in contrast to each other, in a nuanced echo of the more or less ancient movement toward colonization by the Indo-Nepalese founders of the Nation-state of Nepal. In the Gurung and Tamang countries, the situation is even more complex, with traces of the royal authority inspired by the Tibetan model and an implantation of monasteries that appears to have favored the development of a more solid social village unit. With the exception of the Tharu from the plains, the clan or the segment of the clan attached to a territory no doubt preceded the divisions into the "kingdoms," cantons and "villages," which still define the attributions of Bhume today. The complexity of the terminologies still in use suggests, however, a greatly varied regional substratum.

The god Bhume now appears to us more as an administrative god guaranteeing the authority over a registered territory by an external authority than as a god of power. If Bhume bears witness to a former religion of chiefs, it is of chiefs who now have lost the essence of their power over the soil, both forest and untamed areas, in favor of a simple function of managing the land ownership of the "king of kings." The beneficent character of the completely Hinduized god Bhume, favoring the fecundity of the earth more than the power of the soil (a polysemy implicit in the word itself), can be read as a total "pacification" of the untamed forces that once guaranteed the power of the former clan chiefs. This was based on the political and physical division of a territory thereby colonized and sapped of its strength, in favor of the royal Hindu forms of sovereignty.

Notes

1. A. Höfer, "Notes sur le culte du terroir chez les Tamang du Népal," in: J.M.C. Thomas and L. Bernot (eds.), *Langues et techniques, nature et société II: approche éthnologique, approche naturaliste*, Paris, 1971, p. 147.
2. B. Pignède, *Les Gurung. Une population himalayenne du Népal*, Paris-The Hague, 1966, p. 300.
3. J. Kawakita, *The Hills Magars and Their Neighbours*, Tokyo, 1974, p. 343.

4. G. Krauskopff, "Naissance d'un village tharu, à propos des rites de claustration villageois," in: *L'Ethnographie*, Vol. 83, No. 100/1 (1987), pp. 131-58; also in: idem, *Maîtres et possédés, les rites et l'ordre social chez les Tharu (Népal)*, Paris, 1989, pp. 110-17.
5. The Tharu live in the plains bordering India – a region more directly influenced by the popular Hinduism of Northern India. In comparative perspective, it should be noted that among the Reddis of India (see C. von Fürer-Haimendorf, *The Reddis of the Bison Hills*, London 1945) Bhume, who does not have a sanctuary and is clearly identified with the protecting mother earth helping to secure good harvests, stands completely apart from the village goddesses, such as Gangamma Devi and Mutielamma, who by contrast are represented on the outskirts of certain villages through rocks or woodden posts.
6. E. Chavannes, *Le T'ai Chan. Essai de monographie d'un culte chinois* (Annales du Musée Guimet 28), Paris, 1910, pp. 471, 477.
7. V. Bouillier and G. Toffin (eds.), "Classer les dieux? Des panthéons en Asie du Sud," in: *Purusartha*, 15 (1993).
8. See V. Bouillier, "Mahadev himalayen," in: ibid., p. 178.
9. M. Lecomte-Tilouine, "About Bhume. A Misunderstanding in the Himalayas," in: G. Toffin (ed.), *Nepal. Past and Present*, Paris, 1993.
10. Ch. Ramble, "The Founding of a Tibetan Village: The Popular Transformation of History," in: *Kailash*, Vol. X, No. 1 (1983), pp. 279f.
11. B. Pignède (note 2 above), p. 308.
12. V. Elwin, *Bondo Highlanders*, Bombay, 1950, p. 182.
13. M. Oppitz, "The Wild Boar and the Plough. Origin Stories of the Northern Magar," in: *Kailash*, Vol. X, No. 1 (1983), pp. 187-226.
14. M. Lecomte-Tilouine, *Les dieux du pouvoir. Les Magar et l'hindouisme au Népal central*, Paris, 1993.
15. As has been well demonstrated by M. Höfer (note 1 above), p. 147.
16. M. Lecomte-Tilouine (note 14 above), pp. 95-99. See also A. de Sales, *Je suis né de vos jeux de tambours. La religion chamanique des Magar du Nord*, Nanterre, 1991.
17. M. Höfer, *Tamang Ritual Texts I. Preliminary Studies in the Folk Religion of an Ethnic Minority in Nepal*, Wiesbaden, 1981, pp. 26, 36.
18. B. Steinmann, *Les Tamang du Népal; usages et religion, religion de l'usage*, Paris, 1987, p. 172.
19. M. Gaborieau, "Introduction," in: idem (ed.), *Caste, lignage, territoire et pouvoir en Asie du Sud*, *L'Homme*, Vol. 18, No. 1/2 (1978), p. 23.
20. The system of the Panchayats represented a radical reversal from the principle of universal suffrage to elect the *pancayat*, the village committee, and its head, the *pradhan panc*. Previously, the chiefs had been nominated by the central government. The village units were redrawn and divided into wards. With the exception of a brief democratic period, the system of the Panchayats followed the autocratic regime of the Rana and was abolished in the "revolution" of 1990 that resulted in the return to political parties and to the election of a parliament on the basis of the universal suffrage.
21. See M. Höfer (note 17 above), p. 10.
22. Ph. Sagant, "Le pouvoir des chefs limbu au Népal oriental," in: *L'Homme*, Vol. 18, No. 1/2 (1978), pp. 69-107.

23. However, harvest cults and in order to "satisfy the earth" (*yoba-tama*) are being held twice per year under the guidance of *subba* (in fact corresponding to a group of houses belonging to a segment of the clan): they reunite the men of the clan and are performed by the "tribal high priest" on temporary altars. They involve an atonement of the forest spirits to "enclose the land" and among the Sansari to keep out epidemics. During sowing time, they allow the "power of the grain" to assure abundance. I thank Ph. Sagant for giving me this information.
24. N.J. Allen, "The Thulung of the Bhume Sites and Some Indo-Tibetan Comparisons, " in: C. von Fürer-Haimendorf (ed.), *Asia Highland Societies in Anthropological Perspective*, New Delhi, 1981, pp. 168-82.
25. C. MacDougall, *The Kulunge Rai. A Study in Kinship and Marriage Exchange*, Khatmandu, 1979, p. 33.
26. M. Gaenzle, "Ancestral Types: Mythology and the Classification of 'Deities' among the Mewahang Rai," in: V. Bouillier and G. Toffin (eds.) (note 7 above), pp. 197-218.
27. B. Pignède (note 2 above), p. 45.
28. M. Gaborieau (note 19 above), pp. 37-67.
29. Ph. Ramirez, *Patrons et clients. Etudes des relations politiques sur le site d'un ancien royaume indo-népalais, Argha (Népal central)*, PhD. thesis, University of Paris X, 1993, p. 265.
30. The Kali Gandaki basin where the "Twenty-Four" Hindu kingdoms existed in the fifteenth and sixteenth centuries is also known as "Magar country" (*magarant*) or in certain documents as *magar visaya*, occasionally also as *bara magarant* ("the twelve magar countries"). Our knowledge is poor as to how the succession among local chiefs and Hindu chiefs worked: marriage alliances or political alliances; military conquest or elevation of the head of a clan to the position of "Hindu king." It is possible to think of a variety of scenarios.
31. N. J. Allen (note 24 above) pp. 169-72.
32. B. Steinmann (note 18 above), p. 90.
33. This is the Tharu term for identifying land not owned by anyone.

The Cult of the Earth Goddess Among the Magar of Nepal

Marie Lecomte-Tilouine

The military conquest of the Magarant, the Magar land, took place during the sixteenth and seventeenth centuries, when the Thakuri petty kings and their dependents (priests, artisans, soldiers) fled India to settle there. The Magar resistance appears to have been weak, due to their lack of unity and the alliances the conquerors formed with some of them. The Magar people quickly opted for assimilation into the royal caste of the Thakuri, adopting most of their cultural traits, notably their language and religion. Nevertheless they retained or developed particularisms in their relationship to the earth, as we can see in the rites they devote to Bhume. We should emphasize first and foremost that the name Bhume is itself Nepalese, derived from the sanskrit *bhû, bhûmî*. This goddess is neglected by the Hindi of high caste, whereas she is central to the Magar. This paradox has two possible sources: the Magar might have identified one of their principal goddesses with a minor Hindu deity by virtue of a common relation to the earth, conferring an unusual importance on the latter. Or they might have constructed a divine being on the basis of Hindu concepts, as the result of a new-found need to defend their rights to the earth in the face of the Hindu invaders. The second hypothesis seems more likely, since there is no trace of a Magar earth goddess before Bhume. Even in the regions where the Magar retained the use of their original language (such as in Palpa, Syangja, or in the Kham country) and where, consequently, some of the gods have Magar names, the earth goddess is called by Nepalese terms, such as Bhume, Bhuyar, or Bhayar. Furthermore, even if the Magar themselves once had an earth goddess of their own, the renaming of this deity would indicate a change of identity, given the importance of a divinity's name.

There are other indications that tend to support the idea that the goddess Bhume was developed as a reaction to the conquest. For example, the Magar call themselves autochthonous and freely describe themselves as "elders by the earth," an expression that was obviously created afterwards, and rests on the idea of linking ancestrality and power over the earth, two cental aspects of Magar identity. The precedence of their settlement of the land, as well as their martial character, in point of fact earned the Magar the relatively noble position of lower Kshatriyas in the new society created during the sixteenth and seventeenth centuries. The precedence of their settlement is an indication of prestige among the Magar – who never tire of flaunting it – as well as in a caste society that recognizes it. And in fact the Magar easily found a Hindu deity, Bhume, upon which to graft an ideology that equated rights to the earth with ancestrality, placing the people of high caste, the more recently installed Hindi, in a delicate position, analogous *mutatis mutandis* to that of the Aryans in tribal India. As the example of the Magar in Nepal demonstrates, the earth cults and the monopoly of the priesthood over the earth deities can reflect a reaction to an invasion rather than a set primitive tradition. Confronted by people who flaunted their superiority in terms of purity, the Magar responded with a faint echo that claimed themselves elders by the earth and thus deserving of respect. The link between power and ancestrality, on the other hand, which is clearly illustrated in the Magar sense of the word *mijar*, meaning both elder of the founding line and the head of the village, and which underlies the cult of Bhume, was not recognized by the people of higher caste.

Bhume in the Local Pantheon of Gulmi

In a polytheism as richly developed as that of central Nepal, where Hindu and Magar cultures (to cite but the two cultures under examination here) are inextricably bound, the gods often lack distinct traits, and their functions are not clearly defined. Their nature can nevertheless be gleaned through their various associations, which are expressed verbally or made manifest in rites. This is why I consider Bhume a special case in their pantheon; in some ways she is like an evil forest spirit, in others she shares certain characteristics with the great masters of the earth, the mountain ridge gods.

Of the three levels that make up the world, the earth is the one shared between man, "the kings of cultivated lands," and the "petty deities," the "forest kings." This realm is ruled from on high by celestial gods residing on the mountain tops, the "Kailash" gods, who govern the whole earth (*prtvi*) as well as the great natural phenomona such as rain, hail, and epidemics. Associated with asceticism, these gods are nonetheless described as owners of the earth, such as Malika, whose name means "the owner." Identified with extreme purity, their worship is reserved for the society's elite, the Indo-Nepalese high caste and, to a lesser extent, the Magar. They are inaccessible to low castes and to women.

As we have mentioned, the men and their ruling deities share the earthly level with "forest" spirits. In this world the forest includes water, roads, and the underworld. The earth and the underground are part of the same level, and the gods found there are often described as evil spirits or forest deities. Bhume herself is conceived as such, but her position is unique; a wild goddess domesticated by man, she sides not with her own kind, but with the villagers who nurture and honor her. Her ties to the forest, where violent death prevails, are nevertheless emphasized by the fact that she is often described as the goddess of death. We cannot see this as a characteristic of an indigenous Magar earth goddess, dating from before the concept of Bhume, because relations between the deceased and Bhume are also found both among the caste peoples in central Nepal and in popular Indian Hinduism.

Men and forest deities are competitive and malevolent to one another. The main difference between them is a knowledge of agriculture, possessed by man and unknown to all others. These forest divinities are much like hunter-gatherers, living on predation. In fact, the groups of hunter-gatherers on their way to extinction, such as the Raute or the Kusunda, are imagined as forest divinities in central Nepal. When they offer up a prayer to the forest divinities, the men begin by offering them precisely what they lack, such as small shelters, the replica of movable sheds, as well as a miniature technical panoply (bow and arrows, a drum, kitchen paddles, yeast), and, in particular, an ensemble of agricultural tools (hoe, swing-plough, beam, plane, etc.)

The Representation of Ploughing

Of all these agricultural tools, the swing-plough is held in the highest regard. It is the only tool to which people offer a prayer before using it, and the one that represents the highest achievement of their culture.[1] This is because the use of the plough not only distinguishes man from the spirits, it also defines a territory, and likewise a property. Thus up until the 1960s, non-cultivated private land was not considered the sole property of the owner. For example, in the village of Darling (Gulmi) where I stayed, anyone could gather fodder or firewood there. In similar fashion, itinerant farming did not correspond to ownership. It was only after three years of working the same spot that someone was expected to pay taxes, and in this way assumed ownership. In the many regions of Nepal, such as the Terai or the Mahabharata, the boundaries of the locality or properties are marked by ploughshares driven into the earth. While ploughing distinguishes man, as a peasant, from the errant spirits living by predation, which is to say from the spirits on this side of the divine, it also separates him from the other-worldy divine, those who inhabit the world of gods. Indeed, contact with the earth, of which ploughing is the most complete expression, is the lot of the ordinary man; the Hindu gods never touch the earth, and ascetics (or the crowned king) keep their distance from it by wearing wooden sandals. Furthermore, it is written in the Satapatha Brahmana 1.9.1.29 that the sacrificer may reach the heavens through sacrifice, but that if he does not return he risks going mad. To remain human, he must in fact touch the earth. The brahmins, who live on earth in spite of their divine pretensions, nonetheless do not till it; they have neither the right to work the land nor to enter it for its exploitation, such as entering a mine, for example.

The passing of the plough has an important sexual symbolism. Valued for both its virile aspect and for the fact that this activity requires great skill – it is one of the only manual labors in which men are proud to be photographed – it also represents, in Hindu terms, an impure blot that might taint a man of high caste. Sexuality and impurity in fact characterize both ploughing and its fruits. People say that in order to avoid all contact with cultivating the land – but might this not rather be with sexuality? – ascetics traditionally do not eat the fruits of ploughing, while brahmins living in the world content themselves with avoiding the touch of the plough. Moreover, nubile women, in anticipation of the day of *rsi pancami* – a ritual during which they purify themselves of their menses and recover their virginity – turn up small plots with hoes and eat pure rice in the furrow. The homology between earth and woman, between ploughing and the resulting sexual relationships, is taken even further in certain regions of India such as Bengal, where men stop ploughing and having carnal relations with their wives during a ritual period of five days corresponding to the "earth's menstruations," a taboo one also finds in Nepal, during a day set aside "to avoid the earth." Significantly, the virgin and wild goddesses of central Nepal, such as Malika, must not be offered products of the fields, while people must abstain from eating grains on the day of their worship. The sexual symbolism of the plow can again be found in a ritual practiced by the shamans of Gulmi. This consists of being rid of the spirit of a still-born child or a child who died young by sealing it into an earthenware pot, which symbolizes a womb, the opening of which stoppered by a swing-plough before it is buried at a crossroads.

By the passing of the swing-plough, man thus enters into a special relationship with the earth. Here I am speaking of man with a small letter "m," since women are excluded from the cults pertaining to the fertility of the fields and the earth in general. She is not supposed to step over the swing-plough or even an ox harness. As we see, the swing-plough belongs to the realm of the masculine in the face of the feminine, to humanity and the cultivated world in the face of untamed spirits and gods.

The Earth

The earth is ambivalent. It contains an intrinsic power that regenerates both men and demons. In the myth of the struggle between the first shaman and the nine witch sisters in the Gulmi region, the shaman is vanquished by the sorceresses, who rip out his heart and roast it. The shaman nonetheless succeeds in eating his own heart and falls into a transe, declaring that he will "entrust himself to the earth." He lies down flat on his stomach on the ground for seven days, at the end of which he is reborn in all his glory. The power recognized in the earth can also be found among the Kham Magar, who call the ceremony they devote to Bhume a "ritual of power."[2] Its principle of vital energy is quite often the trump of demons, who come back to life or multiply in contact with the earth, as does Raktabija. Although the earth contains a formidable energy, the passage of the plough is considered an extenuating activity, the only one for which in the end the laborers are for the most part compensated for their efforts. The ambivalence of the earth can also be found in the myth of Prthu. Usually depicted in Hindu mythology as a defenseless woman oppressed by too heavy a load, who begs the gods or the king to come to her assistance, the earth appears in this myth as a perfidious creature who swallows all the vegetation herself and causes the world to waste away.

In short, the ambiguous nature of the earth is related to purity. As opposed to elements such as fire, which nothing can deprive of its pure character, the earth absorbs impurity, purifying it, while it is also capable of becoming tainted or contaminated. Hence women of high caste can be seen washing themselves with earth, then avoiding contact with it once purified by sitting on a banana leaf and not on the ground during the rite of *rsi pancami*.

We can identify two different male attitudes toward these ambivalent aspects of the earth, which I would call "brahmin" and "royal" respectively. The former is respectful. One finds this attitude among the brahmins of Gulmi, who make sure they do not plough so as not to "wound their mother," the earth, or among the Maharastra, who excuse themselves each morning before beginning to plough. The second attitude is much more complicated, as the myth of Prthu, mentioned above, bears witness. The king, generally depicted as the protector of the earth, here appears to dominate it. Earth had swallowed the vegetation and allowed the world to waste away, until Prthu forced it to return its bounty, leveled it out, and founded agriculture. In the Mahabharata or the

Bhagavata Purana, Prthu is thus described as the father of the earth, but this filiation is not so firmly established since the Laws of the Manou describe him as her husband. In fact, there are many indications that the king enters into a very intimate relationship with her, both protecting and dominating her, and that he is conceived of as her ploughman and husband.

In classical mythology, the earth goddess Bhume is a young woman of great beauty, is in danger. She plunges into the depths of the ocean. He who will save her is in fact the prototype of the ploughman, a wild boar. Let us remember that the wild boar digs the earth with his tusks to hunt for roots and that in the myths of central Nepal, it is often on land dug up by a wild boar in this fashion that a hunter sows seed and founds a village. It is significant that the Hindu kings often identify themselves with the wild boar, saving, working, and loving the earth. The deep intimacy between the Hindu kings and the earth is expressed through the Nepalese royal consecration, marked by anointing the king's body with earth from the different parts of the kingdom, while this unction is compared to a union. Moreover, the king is frequently called Bhupati (in the national hymn for example), the master or husband of the earth.

The privileged relationship that unites the sovereign with the earth can likewise be seen in the belief held among some of the Magar, according to which the king of Nepal would plough each year, followed by the queen, sowing the seeds. This ritual is thought to take place every year in the beginning of spring, opening the agricultural season. I was not able to verify this, although it seems improbable, since the custom has not lasted up to the present time. Whether or not the king of Nepal ploughs is of little importance, since this belief underlines the strict tie between the king and the earth's fertility in the eyes of the villagers. And the king radically distinguishes himself from his peers in this act (or in the belief of the existence of this act), which is forbidden to the brahmins and the Thakuri. We do have a famous example of royal labor in the Ramayana, when Sita is born from the earth when king Janaka makes a furrow with his swing-plow, and the custom has been verified at least in the ancient Indianized royal kingdom of Cambodia. Faced with the brahmin's respectful attitude toward the earth, imagined as a descending filiation, the king, her protector, demonstrates his dominination over her; he is either her father or husband, and not her son. The Mahabharata 13.8.21 clearly establishes the privileged relation between the earth and warriors, without, however, explaining why the brahmins are "absent": "In the case when the husband is absent (dead), the wife marries his younger brother. In this way, since the earth cannot have a brahmin, she takes a Kshatriya to wed."

Let us now examine the agrarian rites that punctuate the agricultural cycle in the Gulmi region, before examining the collective cults offered to the earth gods, who on this level are imagined as the protectors of a territory in connection with power.

Offerings to Bhume and the Earth Deities

The three main crops cultivated in the district of Gulmi are rice, corn and eleusine. The oldest of the three crops is eleusine, but this grain for the poor is considered impure, and its first fruits are rarely offered to Bhume. To my knowledge, only the inhabitants of the village of Darling offer four liters of eleusine to the goddess after its harvest. The cultivation of corn probably dates back to the seventeenth century in Nepal, and its first fruits are offered in most of the villages and among all the groups. The ceremony is simple. The divinity is represented by a stone in the field and is usually accompanied by Nag and Nageni, a couple of divine snakes, and Jhankri, the shaman of irrigated lands, as well as Sikhari, the divine huntress. A chicken is often sacrificed, then a libation of milk and fumet of clarified butter mixed with artemisia are offered to the deities. Afterwards, a whole cornstalk is uprooted and the officiating priest, opening the husks, places it on Bhume's altar, "ready to be eaten." One ear is then grilled on the hearth, then a few kernels are mixed with butter and offered in three vessels intended, respectively, for Bhume, the divinities of the lineage and the "divinities of the outside." More simply, the brahmins of the village of Musikot, for example, content themselves with alerting Bhume that they are going to harvest the field with this phrase: "Very well, now we are going to eat grains."

Aside from these widespread offerings of first fruits, the villagers from Darling offer four litres of corn in the name of Bhume after the harvest, but here again they are an exception.

The offering of four liters is most often made when only rice is cultivated. The offering is presented to a young virgin girl in each household in the name of Bhume. The young girl disposes of it as she sees fit, eating it, selling it, or even making it into alcohol if her caste allows it and she desires to do so. This offering indicates that Bhume is conceived of as daughter of the head of the household. This is unusual, for it is not a question of food left over from an offering to the gods or a sacrificial wage; the young girl is substituted for the goddess herself, as recipient of the offering. The worship of Bhume also accompanies the cutting of paddy. It takes place on the threshing floor or in the field and usually includes the sacrifice of chickens.

Aside from these agrarian rites, two similar ceremonies in which Bhume, Jhankri, Nag and Sikhari are worshiped take place in the months of November and December (*mansir*) and April and May (*baisakh*). During these times, both a compensation and a restitution are offered to the earth deities. Therefore the brahmins of the village of Asleva leave a little chicken in the fields so that it may go into the forest and become wild. In exchange for the fruits of cultivated earth, man gives nature a small domesticated animal, in order to maintain an equilibrium between the wild and the cultivated, as if to appease the wild side of Bhume.

As we can see, it is mostly harvesting that prompts the worship of Bhume. This includes three other deities in the agricultural context. First of all is Sikhari, the forest deity presiding over wild animals and the hunt. The relationship between Sikhari and Bhume can be seen in the village of Neta, in the commune of Dibrung, where the Magar offer the heart, liver, and rissoles of meat of the slaughtered game to Bhume (in her dual guise of Sime-Bhume) in place of Sikhari. The second deity accompanying Bhume is Jhankri. Jhankri is a generic term that designates, in the region of Gulmi, the forest divinities related to shamanism. Bhume herself sometimes qualifies as such. Most often, Jhankri or the couple (Jkankri and Jhankreni) who accompany her in the rites preside over the muddy earth, such as irrigated fields, as well as the aquatic element in general. Just as Bhume appears to the Magar in dreams in the guise of a young and beautiful brahmin's daughter, decked out in finery and dark-complexioned, Jhankri is imagined as a rich man with black skin. More than Bhume, he is a *lago*, a god who sends calamities. A Magar once told me that after having ploughed his irrigated fields he saw two beautiful women with dark complexions walking in it. The next day he fell ill and concluded that he had seen Jhankri's wives, who had sent him his illness. An irrigated field is considered dangerous. The Dogmani Gharti Magar of Darling thus imagine that one of their ancestors died in his irrigated field when he tried to plough it, sinking into the mud with his oxen, where he remains to this day. Jhankri is the counterpart of Bhume, her complement. Bhume herself is often called Sime-Bhume, although Sime, whose name means "the one from muddy ground, from the source," never appears as an individual entity. Their inseparability serves as a reflection. Hence a Kami artisan from Darling explained to me one day that the Kami and the Magar were like Sime-Bhume, inseparable and complementary.

Finally, the last divine figure associated with Bhume is Nag, the divine snake living in the underworld. Like Bhume and Jhankri, the Nags appear as bearers of wealth, and this trait should be considered characteristic of the earth and all those who inhabit it, particularly in the region where mineral lodes are plentiful. Here again there are strong ties between Bhume and the Nags. Their figures are, it appears, partially confused among the Kham Magar.[3] Likewise, in the village of Darling, one day someone said to me that "they were making a snake of ashes for Bhume," without it being clear whether the snake represented the divinity or was being offered to her.

Nag plays a special role in the agricultural cycle. He is the object of a well-known cult in the Hindu world, the *nag pancami*, which falls on the fifth day of the somber two-week period of *saun*, in June and July. On this occasion, all over Nepal and in the north of India, people paste drawings of Nag onto the doors of houses and temples. In Darling, people say this day is the day that Nag and all the other snakes emerge and rise out of the ground. For the villagers it is also the beginning of winter, which corresponds indeed to the "descending season" (*udauli*), the season during which the sun begins its trajectory toward the north. The purpose of this ritual is made clearer through comparison with what takes place during its counterpart six months later, in *sri pancami*, in the beginning of spring and the rising season (*ubhauli*). People say *sri pancami* marks the beginning of cultivation. Each person must plough his field or have it ploughed. The first cut of the plough is ritualized. First the "snake is scaled," then "split," and then "cut into pieces." The placing of this snake in the field is determined by an astrological computation, and the ploughman must take special care to scale the snake by beginning with the tail. With the snake thus cut into pieces, the field becomes "homogeneous." The presence of the snake in the earth is an obstacle to working the field and especially to the working of the swing-plough; they compete. Once scattered, "there are Nags everywhere, in a continuous fashion," people say, and working the fields may begin. The snake regulates the solar and agricultural calendar. Killed for the rising season and working the fields, it is reborn in the descending season to protect the crops as they ripen. The main role the villagers attribute to the Nag is to protect the crops from thieves and evil spirits. The role of protecting the crops is also an attribute of Bhume. It is taken much further in the case of the latter, since she assures the protection of the men who cultivate the fields. Thus a young Magar, frightened to see me walking around the village at night, told me that if I encountered an evil spirit, I would be advised to jump off the road and into a field where Bhume would protect me. The protection is better, he added, if the field belongs to you, which underscores the contract that independently links each domestic group with the form of the goddess presiding over his lands.

Akin to the forest deities and to those of the underground, Bhume appears as the daughter of the head of the household at the time of the offerings of the first fruits. This idea, which is linked to the "brahminic" attitude toward the earth, coexists with the idea that the chief, or *mukhiya*, can be substituted for the goddess. This is indicated, for example, in the symbolic purchase of a tomb site near Bhume, an act usually performed with the chief. In this the Magar chief is no different from the Hindu king, often described as akin to the earth.

The Village Cults Dedicated to Bhume

Intimately linked to the founding of a village, the cult of Bhume remains associated with the first settlers. Most often it is conferred through tribal lineage. In the village of Aglung, the inhabitants go so far as to hire an officiating priest from a neighboring locality, descendent from a group of Magar who once lived on their lands, and who had been pushed north at the time of the subsequent settlement. Four hundred houses join together for this cult and offer an enormous sacrificial payment to the Magar officiating priest from the village of Kahare Darling, who receives a half-liter of rice from each for his office. Should we see this as a ritual compensation, guaranteed by Bhume, for lost lands?

The collective cults dedicated to Bhume are intimately tied to power and political units. Bhume is an omnipresent deity, defined by the sociological group that worships her. Hence in Darling one speaks of the "Bhume of each man's field," who are the recipients of the agrarian rites I mentioned, as well as the "Bhume of the whole village." One finds this distinction among the Magar of Sikha who recognize on the one hand a Mukhiya Bhume, the deity of the territory of the chief, or *mukhiya*, who is worshiped by the chief who "protects the people, the crops and prevents epidemics," and, on the other hand, a *"thum* Bhume," belonging to a vast political unit comprised of many territories of *mukhiya*. In Sikha, over and above individual and village cults, there exist territorial cults devoted to Bhume.[4]

Conversely, in the district of Gulmi, the cult of Bhume is often based on very small territorial units, such as the *tol* (quarters), or the *ward*, administrative divisions of the Panchayat. This can probably be explained by the fact that the Magar are less numerous there. Hence, in a Panchayat such as Badagaon, in Gulmi, where the population is largely made up of people in castes, only the Magar hamlet organizes a collective cult of Bhume. In many Magar villages, the officiant of the collective cult of Bhume was the chief, or *mukhiya*, up until the reform of the Panchayats in 1961. This cult, intimately tied to political organization, changes considerably with each political reform. Before examining its evo-

The Village Cults Dedicated to Bhume

Intimately linked to the founding of a village, the cult of Bhume remains associated with the first settlers. Most often it is conferred through tribal lineage. In the village of Aglung, the inhabitants go so far as to hire an officiating priest from a neighboring locality, descendent from a group of Magar who once lived on their lands, and who had been pushed north at the time of the subsequent settlement. Four hundred houses join together for this cult and offer an enormous sacrificial payment to the Magar officiating priest from the village of Kahare Darling, who receives a half-liter of rice from each for his office. Should we see this as a ritual compensation, guaranteed by Bhume, for lost lands?

The collective cults dedicated to Bhume are intimately tied to power and political units. Bhume is an omnipresent deity, defined by the sociological group that worships her. Hence in Darling one speaks of the "Bhume of each man's field," who are the recipients of the agrarian rites I mentioned, as well as the "Bhume of the whole village." One finds this distinction among the Magar of Sikha who recognize on the one hand a Mukhiya Bhume, the deity of the territory of the chief, or *mukhiya*, who is worshiped by the chief who "protects the people, the crops and prevents epidemics," and, on the other hand, a *"thum* Bhume," belonging to a vast political unit comprised of many territories of *mukhiya*. In Sikha, over and above individual and village cults, there exist territorial cults devoted to Bhume.[4]

Conversely, in the district of Gulmi, the cult of Bhume is often based on very small territorial units, such as the *tol* (quarters), or the *ward*, administrative divisions of the Panchayat. This can probably be explained by the fact that the Magar are less numerous there. Hence, in a Panchayat such as Badagaon, in Gulmi, where the population is largely made up of people in castes, only the Magar hamlet organizes a collective cult of Bhume. In many Magar villages, the officiant of the collective cult of Bhume was the chief, or *mukhiya*, up until the reform of the Panchayats in 1961. This cult, intimately tied to political organization, changes considerably with each political reform. Before examining its evolution, I will describe, as an example, the cult I was able to observe in 1990 in Syaulibang (the district of Pyuthan), where the former *mukhiya* continues to exercise his role of officiant as in the past.

Some time before the offering, each household under the *mukhiya*'s control sends him a half-liter of corn with which he makes beer. Then, three days before the offering, he presents himself to the Bhume's sanctuary, where he remains alone, day and night. The villagers take turns bringing him his meals there. These meals must include a fish, supposedly the first catch of the year. The offering takes place on the tenth day of the bright month of *mansir* (November and December), at the beginning of winter and the fishing season. Hence at one time it opened the season of hunting, since an animal killed in the forest was supposed to be brought to the *mukhiya* at the same time as the fish. In the sanctuary, the *mukhiya* may not speak during his close confinement; no one may even touch his house. When he returns home on the morning of the offering, he sprinkles his way with holy water in order to remain pure. He sits on a leaf on the veranda of his house, wearing a white turban on his head, still without speaking. All the villagers gather in his courtyard, bearing rice as well as kids and sheep offered as pledges of sacrifice to the deity. Damai musicians play their instruments, to which strips of cloth have been hung. A man from the *mukhiya*'s lineage officiates as priest. He takes the twelve jars of beer from the chief's house and places them in the courtyard. Then he measures the rice brought by each person into a large cloth placed on the ground, verifying that each family has indeed brought a half-litre, and places it all in a basket. The chief gives orders with gestures of his hands and head. He designates the priests and the Damai, signalling for them to leave. They go straight to the sanctuary, where the priest offers incense, milk and strips of cloth to Bhume. The chief then points to a man in the crowd who carries a bow and quiver. He comes to the center of the courtyard and executes a very beautiful dance, flourishing his drawn bow. Turning slowly, he removes an arrow from the quiver and pretends to shoot it in the four directions of the universe. With a wave of his hand the *mukhiya* dismisses him. This man is a Bhujel Magar, a wife-taker in the chief's lineage; he leaves to worship Sikhari near a spring. The priest then returns from the sanctuary and the chief orders him to leave again. Seizing the basket containing the rice, he goes back to the sanctuary. Finally the twelve jars of beer are seized by different men, at the *mukhiya*'s command, and brought to the sanctuary (*than*). The chief and the priest then wash themselves in the river and afterwards all the villagers proceed to Bhume's *than*, bearing their sacrificial victims. Only the men have the right to approach the sanctuary, although they do not have the right to go inside. They prepare rice with milk in a large pot, while the *mukhiya*, alone and still silent, takes hold of a large sabre with a flared blade and decapitates the sacrificial victims one by one in a great slaughter, for the animals are not supposed to be attached and no one is allowed to help him. Next comes a banquet in which the entrails of the victims are eaten with milk, rice, and the corn beer offered by the community. Here again, the women do not take part in the feast, which nevertheless unites the men of all castes and notably the Damai, the very low caste of tailor-musicians.

This rite is enacted primarily by the chief. Based on a script well-known to all, since it takes place wordlessly, it stages a pure chief of supreme authority: all the actors obey the slightest nod of his head. One sees clearly the role of the village priest, who is acknowledged as chief among the Magar. During the time of the cult, he enters into an exclusive relationship with the earth goddess, with whom he first spends three days and nights in private conversation, speaking to no one. He finds himself transformed by this intimate contact with the goddess into a state of purity that cuts him off from the rest of the world, since when he emerges from his asceticism he still may not speak to anyone and must particularly avoid contact with the earth, purifying his way with water and sitting on leaves. In short, he is the only one who may penetrate the goddess' sanctuary and offer her sacrifices. This exclusive relationship with the goddess is very unusual in central Nepal, and one can notice the quasi-matrimonial relationship between the *mukhiya* of Syaulibang and Bhume, whom the chief's brother described to me as "our wife" (since the chief himself could not speak to me).

In fact, information from the village of Darling indicates that the "Bhume of the whole village" was once, long ago, merely the

Bhume belonging to the chief. The ritual took place in the very courtyard of his house, where he sacrificed to the goddess, with his own hands, a pig whose flesh was eaten by all the village men, to the exclusion of the women. The purification of the Syaulibang chief no doubt embodies a collective dimension, as does the Darling chief's cult of Bhume. Elsewhere in fact, as in the Kham Magar village studied by A. de Sales,[5] the whole village must be purified before worshipping Bhume, and all the villagers are confined.

For the Magar, the concept of the village community is structured, in part, around the cult of Bhume, in which everyone particpates. In Sikha, where a certain number of people recently settled, the celebration of Bhume defines the "real villagers,"[6] and those who do not participate are not really part of the community. The cult of the goddess combines an ancestral connection to the earth with a recognition of an inherited power over the earth, the power of the *mukhiya*. A Sikha villager thus defines the *jagatko puja* ("cult of territory") in the following, negative terms: "It is different from Bhume because the *mukhiya* does not participate in it; even if he participates, it is as an individual, not as the *mukhiya*."

The strict link between the cult of Bhume and power is seen in the modifications it has undergone as a result of political changes. Thus in Sikha, the cult of the goddess was not carried out in 1960, a date that corresponds to the reform of the Panchayats.[7] J. Kawakita notes: "We stopped giving offerings to Bhume in 1960, because the *mukhiya* took the advice of the younger generation. Unfortunately, this resulted in epidemics, scant crops, and hailstorms in the village. Thus the offering was reinstated in 1960." Similarly, in Darling the reform of the Panchayats had an impact on the *Bhume puja*. Bhume's sanctuary was transferred from the chief's courtyard to the top of the mountain. While it is still the man elected to office by the Panchayat who decides its precise date, he is no longer the officiant of the divinity, but rather a Magar priest. More significantly, the cult of Bhume has been to some extent supplanted by that of a new divine figure, Grama, "the villager," who seems to be for the Panchayat what Bhume was under the *mukhiya*'s jurisdiction.

People in Castes and the Divinity

The attitude of the people in high caste toward the collective cults addressed to Bhume differs according to the context. J. Kawakita discovered that some people refused to participate in a collective cult organized in the territory where they live in the region of Sikha. This extreme attitude seems to belong to the people who have more recently migrated there. In the region of Gulmi, I did not encounter this attitude, and was, on the contrary, struck by the fact that the people of high caste participated in the collective cults of Bhume organized by the Magar, accepting the subordinate role of cook. We must, however, note that this participation took place in contexts in which the Magar were in a majority; but I did discover an extreme case of the organization of a "tribal cult" by people in castes, where there was not a single Magar. The attitude of the high caste toward the Magar Bhume is thus no doubt tied to the conditions of their implantation in their territories. In the former zones of cohabitation, a *modus vivendi* took root, giving a certain prestige to the indigenous people, or allowing them to believe they still had a monopoly of power over the earth.[8]

Regardless of the apparent disinterest in Bhume in the high caste, the religious practices in the district of Gulmi demonstrate that the earth goddess is nevertheless represented in some sanctuaries and receives collective worship in the context the Dasehra festival, during the ten days dedicated to Durga, the warrior form of the goddess. In Dasikot, Rupakot and Juniya, Bhume in fact has a sanctuary in the *kot* (temple arsenal), next to Kadka, the divine sabre. The goddess is represented by a sacred rock driven into the earth. She must remain anchored, as the *kot* in Rupakot demonstrates, where she is situated on the ground floor, while the sanctuary containing the arsenal and the divine sabres is on the first floor. The cult of Bhume still retains an impure connotation in these cases. In Juniya, a Kami officiant (from the lower, artisan caste) offers her chickens, impure animals, that is. In Rupakot she receives chickens as well. The Dasehra, on the other hand, celebrates royal power above all else, through the mediation of the local chief. The very association of Bhume with Khanda, symbol of sovereignty, suggests that for the high caste the only truly divine relationship between a man and the earth is established by the king, of which the local chiefs are but the representatives. Through the cult of Bhume, a direct relation between the chief and the earth takes place among the Magar, while it is mediated by the king among the Indo-Nepalese high caste.

Bhume is the wife of the Magar chief, as she is to the Hindu king. She is the mother (or the virgin daughter) of the Indo-Nepalese of high caste and the ordinary villagers. One might interpret the king's forbidding of brahmins and Thakuri to plough, and severely punishing infractions, as a way of distancing them from direct power over the earth. Nonetheless, while the Hindu king's power over the earth is limitless, except for the ocean, and rests on his military might, the Magar associate power with the first occupation of a territory, thereby restricting it by definition.[9] This idea is obviously bothersome for the high caste immigrants, who arrived after the tribes, seized power, and never ceased to extend it. Thus in the *Gorka Vamshavali*,[10] the lack of enthusiasm for the territorial expansion of the Magar is invoked by two brahmins when they discourage the king, Narabhupal Shah, from taking ministers from this group.

The supremacy of the Hindu king over the earth is nonetheless recognized by the Magar at the time of the Dasai festival. Up until the reform of the Panchayat, the Magar *mukhiya* was doubly legitimized: by a direct relationship to his ancestral land through the cult of Bhume and as a representative of the Hindu king at the time of the Dasai festival. This situation is different from that of the Tibeto-Burmese Limbu peoples from the eastern tip of Nepal, who preserved two concurrent forms of legitimacy after the conquest of their territories: the one delegated by the Hindu king to the Subba chiefs, affirmed by the Dasai festival, and the one conferred upon the former *Hang* chiefs by the power of the mountain.[11] The concentration of these two types of power among the Magar probably goes back to their ancient contacts with the Indo-Nepalese and the alliances their chiefs formed with them. Knowing nothing of the specifically Magar forms of rule before their conquest, the particularisms they cultivate today during the cult of Bhume, in which the chief plays a large role, give us food for thought. Since they were a population of hunters and wandering clearers of the land at their origin, the importance the Magar grant to ploughing lies in contrast to the Limbu ideas of power based on a force of nature. One has the impression that the Magar made a royal Hindu model their own, by rooting it into the earth, in order not to be chased from it. On the other hand, if we refute the idea that the Magar created a later-day ritual in the case of Bhume, the ideas of power over the earth and the source of the chief's power expressed therein manifest great similarities to Hindu thought, which certainly helped in their Hinduization.

Notes

1. Quite often a new plough is put through a little ritual before its first use. Similarly, during the Tihar feast, the plough is the only farm implement that is being venerated. It is decorated with a flower wreath and a *tika* good-luck tag; in the Sallyan, Rolpa and Jajarkot regions the masters of the house take off the plough-share and fill the slade slot with rice.
2. A. de Sales, *Je suis né de vos jeux de tambours*, Nanterre, 1991, p. 93.
3. See M. Oppitz, *Frau für Fron*, Frankfurt, 1988.
4. J. Kawakita, *The Hills Magars and Their Neighbours*, Tokyo, 1974, p. 345. To relativize this statement it should be noted that the *thum* comprise lands of very different sizes depending on the region. In Gulmi they are very large and correspond to those of the ancient kingdoms, and perhaps this explains why they do not have the same rituals.
5. A. de Sales (note 2 above).
6. J. Kawakita (note 4 above), p. 369.
7. At the village level, the reforms of the Panchayats involved a rearrangement of the ancient lands of the *mukhiya* chiefs into larger areas called Gaun Panchayat. Moreover, a person elected by means of the universal suffrage (the Prandhan) replaced the traditional village chiefs whose authority was hereditary.
8. M. Lecomte-Tilouine, "About Bhume. A Misunderstanding in the Himalayas," in: G. Toffin (ed.), *Nepal. Past and Present*, Paris, 1993, pp. 127-34.
9. If the authority of the king in the territories he controlled militarily was not being challenged, his possession of land put him among the Brahmins in Indian history. According to R.C.P. Singh (*Kingship in Northern India*, New Delhi, 1968, pp. 101-10), the Visvakarman Bhauvana myth offers a Brahmin representation of the land that stood opposite to the pretensions of the king.
10. Y. Naraharinath (ed.), *Gorkha Vamshavali*, Benares, p. 101.
11. Ph. Sagant, "Le double pouvoir chez les Yakhthumba," in: G. Krauskopff and M. Lecomte-Tilouine (eds.), *Célébrer le pouvoir. Dasain, une fête royale au Népal*, Paris, 1996.

The Burmese *Nats*
Between Sovereignty and Autochthony

Bénédictine Brac de la Perrière

In Burma, the rituals connected with the earth concern the relationship between the local communities of rice-growers and the political whole that encompasses them. The structure of this totality is a result of the history of the Burmese Buddhist monarchy which was, from the tenth century to the end of the nineteenth, the dominant political institution of the Irrawaddy valley. The Buddhist kings were viewed as the masters of the earth, a role symbolized by the ritual of the first furrow, which they "traced" in the soil in order to inaugurate the work season. Moreover, the native Burmese religious system does not include a deity exclusively associated with the earth and who could, by this right, be the object of a systematic cult. This complex religious system, dominated by Buddhism, includes another cult, that of the thirty-seven *nats*, whose history is linked both to the Burmese monarchical system and the adoption of Theravada Buddhism as the state religion. The fall of the monarchy in 1886 did not bring about its disappearance. On the contrary, this cult is still quite alive and touches all levels of Burmese society. It is especially vibrant in those local communities that worship the thirty-seven *nats* of the national pantheon, viewed as the protector of their land.

The Genesis of the Pantheon: Local Powers and the State

The foundation myth of the *nats* cult attributes the institution of the pantheon of the Thirty-Seven to Anawratha (1044-1077), the first king to establish Burmese dominance over the entire Irrawaddy valley.[1] According to this story, the king initially tried – in vain – to convince the local population, which he had assembled under his crown, to do away with its local religious practices and to convert to Buddhism. Faced with this failure, he decided to take thirty-seven statues, representing the religions practiced at this time, and have them placed around the Shwezigon, the state pagoda, the construction of which had just begun. Although it is difficult to say exactly what the religious practices of this period were, it is likely that the *nats* cult that resulted was of a different kind than the cult that preceded it. Indeed some of the legends concerning the worship of the *nats* ascribe their very existence to a period subsequent to Anawratha's reign, which presumes that the cult did not yet exist in its present form. Whatever the case, it is said that the *nats* were placed under the authority of Thi'dja, the Burmese version of Indra, the king of the Vedic gods. This god, whom the Buddhists call Sakra, is asserted to be the protector of Theravada in Burma. Thus, by the intermediary of Thi'dja, the king made clear the subordination of the former cults to the new state religion, Theravadan Buddhism.

The thirty-six *nats* plus Thi'dja make a pantheon of thirty-seven, a number which corresponds to the sum of 32 + 4 + 1: thirty-two being the number of divinities gathered at Tavatimsa, the city of the Hindu gods, to which Indra, their leader, is added, as well as the four guardians of the orient, called the *lokapala*. The number thirty-seven, which constitutes a cosmogonic category, had been used before the Burmese, by the Pyus and Mons, for the socio-religious organization of the Irrawaddy valley.[2] The thirty-seven *nats* surrounding the Shwezigon pagoda can be taken as the original list of *nats*. Later, the officers of the royal family in fact kept an official list. The last of these, dating from 1805, states that only some of the *nats* lived during the era of Pagan. Thus the original list of *nats* was fundamentally changed after the institution of the pantheon. This list in fact constitutes a catalogue of characters whose identities changed over the course of the centuries and probably never comprised the actual totality of *nats* worshipped in Burma. Thus the number thirty-seven does not correspond to the number of spirits believed to have existed at the time of the creation of the cult: rather it represents another totality, that of the kingdom that the Burmese dynasty was then constructing.

Just like the organization of the cults into an institutionalized pantheon, the nature of the spirits also reflects royal authority. *Nat* is a generic term that can designate Hindu divinities, spirits of nature or of death. The Burmese, however, do not confuse these various categories: *nat* specifically designates the members of the Pantheon of the Thirty-Seven, that is to say, the unfortunate dead and evil spirits who have undergone a transformation intended to make them benevolent. This transformation is brought about by attaching the spirits to an altar. Instituted by the kings, it is similar in form to an act of ritual atonement for an injustice. Indeed, an examination of the legends of the *nats* reveals that they are depicted as rebels or potential rivals of the king, who must rid himself of their presence. However, an unjust or violent death brings not reincarnation, the standard destiny of the Buddhist dead, but rather a potentially dangerous wandering of the soul. The king, in order to lessen the risks that a region exposed to such a form of death might incur, instituted a local cult: he had a temple built, a statue sculpted, and ordered the local population to carry out appropriate rituals.

The elevation of a spirit to the rank of *nat* was the object of a royal decree. As a result, the spirit received the title of sovereign, was installed in a temple called a "palace," and fell under the jurisdiction of the lands received: indeed the role of the *nat* – already recorded in administrative reports in the sixteenth century – is to guarantee that local custom is respected, including the ritual obligations of the local population to it. From the point of view of the monarchy, the cult of the *nats* is thus imposed from above. Yet it is clear that it emanates equally from the local population itself: the monarchy merely channels the local power. In return for respecting the components of the cult and the prohibitions imposed by the *nat*, the local population receives prosperity. This spirit thus becomes the protector of the region in which it rebelled. By transforming it into a *nat*, the king implicitly acknowledges a certain sovereignty for a particular region, or rather, acknowledges a degree of sovereignty in the spirit itself, as if appointing the *nat* a local representative of the royal power. However, from the point of view of the local populace, it is the *nat* who has had his way with the king

This ambiguous position of the *nat*, who – depending on one's point of view – is either imposed by or on the king, finds a parallel in the role of *myo'thou'dji*, or "city head," in the administrative hierarchy. The *myo'thou'dji*, although a hereditary role, must be confirmed both by the royalty and local consensus. However, while the ambiguity of the "city head" is a function of his role as administrative intermediary, the ambiguity of the *nat* is inherent in its very nature. As a subversive force, the *nats* were originally captured and propitiated by the centralizing monarchy, a process that continued until the local *nats* were replaced by others of royal blood. Indeed, with barely a single exception, all the *nats* catalogued on official registers are connected to the reigning dynasties, which contradicts the foundation legend of the cult, stating that it was an expression of autochthonous cults organized by Anawratha. The individual legends indicate that these princely figures were replaced by royalty in the domain that became their own. It must therefore be assumed that these figures were superimposed on ancient local legends, whose motifs they borrowed. Yet this act of appropriation of the *nats*, by identifying the *nats* with royal personages, did not reduce the fundamental duality of the cult itself, which is simultaneously popular and state-sponsored.

Nat, Royalty, and Buddhism

One aspect of this ambivalence is manifested in the role played by the cult in relation to Buddhist worship. Although there can be no confusion or mixture of Buddhist rituals with those addressed to the *nats*, no *nat* ritual can take place outside of a Buddhist context. Indeed the cult of the Thirty-Seven is explicitly designated as that of the "Burmese Buddhists." Moreover, although the cult is situated in a Buddhist context, it is nevertheless inferior to it. This inferiority is embodied both in the different height of Buddhist and *nat* altars, and also by the fact that when a man enters a Buddhist monastery to become a monk, even on a provisional basis, his possession by the *nats* is voided, since the status of bonze confers on its possessor a higher spiritual rank than that of a *nat*. What's more, the bonzes are even forbidden merely to attend a ceremony addressed to a *nat*. This is because the ceremony is perceived as a violation of the principle of detachment advocated by Buddhism.

The depreciation of the cult is justified by the failure of the *nats*, over their history, to live up to Buddhist values, which is confirmed by the very character of the *nats*. At the same time, the transformation these spirits undergo at the moment of their submission to the king implies their integration into the Buddhist value system. This process can be observed in ritual; for example, in the one celebrated at Tauntbyon. The Tauntbyon ritual concerns two brothers, depicted as Muslims, to whom it is forbidden to offer pork and who were executed for refusing to participate in the construction of a pagoda: nevertheless, the ceremony includes an homage to the pagoda paid by these two *nats*. As an extreme case, that of the Lords – a brother and sister – of Prome Lake, the transformation into a *nat* is depicted as a brother's conversion of his sister to Buddhism.

Although the *nats* cult is thus encompassed by Buddhism, it remains a framework within which behavior judged by Buddhism to be deviant or devalued can be expressed in the form of a hitherto disobedient spirit. In such cases, the role of the cult is to treat this deviance. The cult of the *nats*, taken in by Buddhism, thus retains its subversive potential. The non-conformity to values taught by the Enlightened One is in fact an aspect of a rivalry between the local heroes and the royalty; a rivalry expressed on the symbolic level by the submission of the *nats* to Buddhism, and on the political level by their federation in a pantheon, that of the Thirty-Seven. While it is likely that originally this pantheon was only the object of a royal cult, local communities worshipping at that time a limited number of local spirits united in a *nat* that was itself obedient to the royal power. As for the royal power, its strength lay in the concentrated ritual activity – as much centered on Buddhism as on the cult of the *nats* – in regions subservient to the king. The *nats* thus seem not only to be tied to but are an actual expression of the process of Burmese unification; this by the way in which their changing status embodies the absorption of values that can be called autochthonous within the scheme of general values of Burmese Buddhism.

It should also be pointed out that the non-conformity of the *nats* is analogous to the position of the king, in regards to participation in the world. The *nats*, by their actions, oppose the renunciation of the monks just as the king does with his wives, his wealth, his power, and even his long hair. But the king makes up for these demerits inherent in his function by making donations to the monks: this is the basis of their interdependence. For their part, the *nats* can make no such contributions; they cannot accumulate merits as the king does. Instead, by the paradoxes of Buddhist logic, they are trapped in a cycle of interrupted rebirth, unable to get out of it. Still, from the point of view of participation in the material world, the *nats* are in the same position as the king, equally distant from the monks' renunciation of the world.

The local sovereignty of the *nats* is achieved by surrendering the spiritual power they represent. One of the most striking images in the legends is that of a king who, having destroyed his enemy and transformed him into spirit, calls him back to life in a position of homage.[3] He obtains this homage of the spirits by using a scepter given to him by Thi'dja, a divinity of Vedic origin whom we encountered earlier. As the cult's foundation myth states, Anawratha subordinated the Burmese *nats* to Thi'dja, who is of a different nature than they. However, the authority of Thi'dja over the *nats* is only nominal: as the legends tell, Thi'dja intervenes neither in their federation nor in the creation of the *nats*; nor does he intervene in their rituals. In fact, according to the Chronicles, he acts only through the intermediary of the scepter, which he gives to the king with the rest of the royal regalia. As for the exercise of concrete power over the spirits, it is up to the king to keep them respectful and to make *nats* out of them. The king thus appears to fulfill the function attributed to Thi'dja himself in the foundation legend of the cult.

How is this relationship between the king, Thi'dja, and the *nats* to be understood? In the Chronicle Thi'dja is depicted as intervening at the outset of important reigns to hand over the instruments of royal power to the new sovereign. Significantly, he does so for Duttabaung, the first king of Sri Ksetra. This city, which was the capital of the Kingdom of Pyu and located in the central plain of Irrawaddy, was the immediate predecessor to the Kingdom of Burma. In this episode, which was a founding one for the Burmese, who were laying claim to the Pyu legacy, Thi'dja directs the construction of the city, crowns the king, and bestows the instruments of power that will permit, without a blow being struck, the collection of tributes and taxes from the dependent states. In short, he establishes the monarchy. Later, Thi'dja bestows upon one of the legendary kings of Pagan, Pyusawti, the instruments necessary to overcome the kingdom's enemies. Then he gives to Anawratha the scepter that confers upon him the power to control spirits. And this is to mention only the most important actions of this divinity. The Burmese king, without being himself divinized or absorbed by Thi'dja, nevertheless owes his sovereignty to him.

Nonetheless, this sovereignty is only guaranteed when the pretender to the throne benefits from the karma of the Buddhist king and behaves as such. According to the Chronicle, Thi'dja only intervenes for those who, without necessarily being heirs to the throne, possess the inherent virtues of a Buddhist king. Moreover, once they have exhausted their good karma, or if they violate the code of Buddhist virtue, their sovereignty is taken from them. Thus, in the Chronicle, the instruments that Thi'dja conferred on Duttabaung lose their power over his subject populations because of the king's illegitimate confiscation of a religious good. It is at moments like these that the king loses his control over the spirits, which allows them to turn against him: Anawratha's death is an example of this phenomenon.[4] The king-*nat* relation is thus reversible. It is in this context that the full ambivalence of the *nats* becomes manifest: while their subversive potential is unleashed when Buddhist legitimacy, guaranteed by Thi'dja, is lacking, this potential is controlled by the king when legitimacy is present.

Thi'dja therefore has a complex function. It should be recalled, in this context, that he is Indra, that is to say the king of the gods, and, because of his mount, the white elephant Airavata, he is also associated with magical fertility and rain, simultaneously ensuring prosperity and the cosmic order. As such, he confers legitimacy on Burma in two distinct ways: as protector of Buddhism and as master of local spirits, the latter through magic. These two aspects, karmic legitimacy and the power of magic, correspond to the two faces of the personality of the Buddhist sovereign; that of the protector of Buddhist dharma, and that of the conqueror. These two aspects are already contained in the life of the Buddha:

renouncing royalty in order to seek salvation, he teaches the means of obtaining it. The Buddhist monarch assumes an inverse and provisional renunciation, i.e. he is the king who gives up nirvana. Thus, in spite of his good karma, he takes upon himself the inherent defects of the royal condition in order to safeguard the Buddha's teachings. From the point of view of the Burmese royalty, it is Thi'dja who coordinates these two aspects, by making karma the power that confers legitimacy on the king's rule, Thi'dja makes it possible for the king to exercise concrete power.

It should be noted that, although the opposition "of the world"/"out of the world," which characterizes the king/monk relationship, is mediated by Thi'dja, Thi'dja himself does not personally exercise his functions of sovereign of the Burmese *nats* (he leaves these functions to the king), thereby occupying a median position from the point of view of participation in the world. Finally, this account of the model of mutual relations in force among elements of the Burmese royalty shows that the *nats* play the role of intermediary in the symbolic chain of authority linking Thi'dja to the local communities. The king's actions come as if from the outside, since his power is legitimized by values that are themselves external, that is to say the values of Buddhism.

The Burmese and Thai Cases in Perspective

The interdependence that simultaneously separates and unites the king to the monks has often been portrayed as the defining relation of Buddhist monarchies. This emphasis has tended to understate the importance of the relationship between monarchy and local authority, the effect of which has been to blur the particularities of each monarchy. However, P. Mus has already underscored the importance of "the overlap between royal power and its judicial apparatus with the local fabric, rich in territorial cults and non-written practices."[5] Thus, the study of the totality of relations uniting the king, monks, and *nats* reveals that there existed in Burma an institutional interface linking the powers conferred by Buddhism to the temporal authority: the person of Thi'dja/Indra. It would seem that by comparing the different ways that this overlap, an essential element of the system, was constructed, we can begin to characterize the various Buddhist monarchies. How then does this overlap manifest itself in Royal Thai Buddhism?

The Cakri dynasty, currently reigning in Bangkok, uses an Emerald Buddha as its palladium. This jewel, sculpted from a semi-precious stone, is located in the sanctuary of the royal palace and has been studied by numerous commentators, most notably F. Reynolds and S. J. Tambiah, who have interpreted the legend associated with the statue as being an affirmation of the specificity of Royal Thai Buddhism.[6] This legend includes a Burmese episode in which Anawratha "forgets" about the Emerald Buddha from Ceylon,[7] thereby emphasizing the variety of ritual forms then practiced in Pagan; for example, with the arrival of the Buddhist Canon in the eleventh century, a cult of the *dharmaraja* (the dharmic king) arose, while at the same time in Angkor the cult of the *devaraja* was practiced. This difference is expressed in the separation, during a voyage to Southeast Asia, of the *Triptaka* from the Emerald Buddha, which had been joined together in Ceylon and corresponded to two aspects of Buddhist religious practice: one emphasizes the Scriptures or teachings of the Buddha as the only object of worship; the other worships relics and images of the Buddha. The Emerald Buddha given to Anawratha was supposedly a copy of another legendary object: the very first representation of Buddha, made from a gem that Sakra (Indra) had supplied to the Buddhist king Milinda and which is associated with the figure of Cakkravartin, the Buddhist Universal Emperor. This kind of representation was thus already associated with the Buddhist monarchy in Ceylon, which explains why a copy of it was given to Anawratha.

The Emerald Buddha, which legend reported as having been stranded in Angkor, reappears on the historical scene in the sixteenth century, at Chiang Mai, then capital of a Thai kingdom. As it was in Ceylon, the Emerald Buddha was associated with Buddhist writings. In 1778, the Siamese dynasty of the Thonburi adopted it as their palladium; it is currently housed in the stupa of the ancient palace at Bangkok, along with a copy of the *Triptaka*. S. J. Tambiah, in his analysis, ascribes the reuniting of the statue and texts at Chiang Mai to the synthesis of two currents of influence, which began in Siam at the beginning of the sixteenth century: one emanated from Pagan, the other at Angkor.

The legend of the Emerald Buddha therefore bears witness to an awareness, on the part of Thai culture, of a common history linking the Theravadan states of Southeast Asia; although the two forms of Buddhism, Theravada and Mahayana, were known before the eleventh century, it was during this period that for the first time the Sinhalese form of Buddhist royalty, which would determine the politico-religious history of the entire region (the sole exception being Vietnam), was adopted. At the same time, the legend, as told in the Thai Chronicle, served to affirm the specificity of the Siamese form of monarchy; this form, which was more in accord with the Theravada monarchy of Ceylon, its model of origin, conferred a certain preeminence upon Siam in relation to its neighbors. And it was the Emerald Buddha that especially crystallized this specificity.

F. Reynolds has clearly demonstrated the degree to which this symbol is overdetermined. The Emerald Buddha, carved from a green, translucent stone that is probably jasper, is similar to statues found in the Thai-Lao region. These statues were believed to possess powers attributed to the stone itself. Identified with light, lightening, rain, and fertility, the symbolism of the Emerald Buddha overlapped in part with Indra, the divinity who in fact provided the stone from which the statue was sculpted. The Emerald Buddha also evokes the figure of Cakkravartin, the Universal Emperor, whose adornments he wears. In Thailand, the royal princes recited their oaths of loyalty to the reigning monarch in the presence of this statue. A symbol of the Buddhist monarchy, the statue, which legend says was based on a Sinhalese model, became the symbol of the Thai Buddhist sovereign whose power the statue helped legitimate.

At the time of its appearance in Chiang Mai, the Emerald Buddha was superimposed on the cult of *lak muang*, which was one of the forms of spirit worship common in Thai communities prior to these spirits being organized under the tutelage of Buddhist royalty. The *lak muang* ("pillar-principality") was the spirit of the chief's ancestor, to whom the chief devoted a personal cult. This spirit was differentiated from the *phi muang* ("spirit-principality"), which was the tutelary spirit of the land on which the community lived and was the object of collective worship.[8]

The spread of Buddhism to the Thais of Laos and Thailand did not result in the total disappearance of the distinction between *lak muang* and *phi muang*, with its dual ritual orientation, one dynastic and the other territorial. Although it may have been expunged in some areas,[9] F. Reynolds has shown that the worship of the Emerald Buddha, at the time of its introduction in Chiang Mai, was a transference of the worship of the cult of the ancestral lineages of the chiefs of the pre-Buddhist Thai populations. As an embodiment of the Buddhist monarchy in Bangkok, the statue, the king's palladium to which he devotes a private cult, presents itself as the projection of the dynastic aspect of Thai rituality, with the statue being housed in the central stupa which is endowed with territorial signification that is further strengthened by the cosmological structure of this type of building.

If Reynolds' analysis bears up under scrutiny, then it can be affirmed that the dual orientation of rituality in Thai communities, with its combination of ancestral spirits of the chiefs and tutelary spirits, is encountered once more in the symbolic structure of the Thai monarchy, that is to say on a totally different level and furnished with the new values of Buddhism. The dual orientation of this rituality accounts for the distinction of the two principles – that is to say, autochthony and sovereignty – in the political order.[10]

This kind of double orientation in rituality is not present in Burma. The *nats* simultaneously represent autochthony – as emanations of the local communities, which provide the *nats* with their subversive potential – and the local sovereignty that the king is compelled to acknowledge for them on the level of spirituality. As we have seen, the *nats* of the pantheon of the Thirty-Seven are presented as ambivalent, simultaneously tutelary spirits of the local communities and obedient to the sovereign. This is thus a rather different situation than the one found in Thai communities, where the chief's ancestors and later his palladium have a parallel existence to the particular spiritual principle of the local communities.

In my view, this difference accounts for certain specific qualities found in local Burmese cults: notably their arrangement into an integrated pantheon on a national level, which is absent in Thailand; also, on the level of symbolic construction of the royal principle, the absence, in Burma, of a private royal cult dedicated to a statue of Buddha worshipped as a palladium. Finally, while the importance accorded to ancestrality in the definition of royalty among the Thais is revealed in the belief, among non-Buddhist Thais, in the existence of the spirits of ancestral chiefs and in the Emerald Buddha as symbol of the royal dynasty in modern Thailand, this principle is of little general importance for the Burmese and is completely absent in the formulation of ties linking the Buddhist monarchy to local cults.

The Community of Worship: Between Filiation and Locality

Let us return to the king-*nat* relation as it exists in Burma, and to the ritual form of the mandate that the king gives to the *nats*. The most characteristic relation uniting the king to these types of spirits is that of affinity: the king, who is a stranger to the community, imposes his domination on it by taking a wife from among its members, the sister of a *nat*.[11] The taking of a wife, or more exactly, the taking of the sister of a local hero or chief as a wife, implies – in the monarchical language – the submission of this chief to the king. However, in the legends surrounding the *nat*, the king's brother-in-law refuses to submit, in spite of their familial alliance: it is this rebellion that causes his loss and transformation into a *nat*.

These legends of the *nat* communicate – at least in part – the idea that the alliance did not succeed in securing Burmese domination over the local populations. The brother-in-law had thus to be transformed into a *nat*. Also, the queen, sister of the *nat*, does not survive the transformation of her brother. As if she in some sense belongs to him, they join together to form a pair of infertile brother-sister tutelary spirits. Here again, we can see how this pattern is opposed to the model found in Thai communities, where the community's protectors are usually a pair of fertile ancestors.

The absence in Burma of ancestrality in the relations of a community to its territory finds expression in one of the primary modes of ritual worship. As we have seen, each *nat* is, among other things, a tutelary spirit in a region in which he is an object of a special cult practiced by the population in acknowledgment of his belonging to this local community. However, when members of the community move, they bring their cult of origin with them, which they practice in the unity of the extended family and transmit to their descendants. This mode of worship is called *yoya*, which literally means "by the bone." Although it is not subject to rules acknowledged by all, research data show that the eldest of a sibling group tends to be responsible for the cult of the parents at their death: in the case of exogamic marriage from the point of view of the region as the unity of the cult, the son tends to guarantee the continuation of the cult of the father while the eldest daughter does the same for the mother.

The variability of the criteria determining whether one belongs to a particular cult, of the relationship between residency and descent, is, at first glance, troubling. It arises when the fact of belonging to a local community is disturbed, which occurs frequently in the urban milieu. In such cases, the cult seems less concerned with assuring the prosperity of the local soil to which one belongs than it is with being an identity cult. When this identity has been abandoned or forgotten, which is often the case, a person turns to a medium who will search among the *nats* to find the one who is the client's *yoya*. In such cases, the emphasis is on the equivalence of the *yoya* and the origin of the person. However, these assertions, which accord with the ideology of the cult, do not stand up to the systematic survey of these cults that I carried out in the suburbs of Rangoon. My survey revealed a recurring and stereotypical pattern in which the Buffalo Mare of Pegu was identified with the *yoya* of the mother, and the Lord of the White Horse with the *yoya* on the father's side. This configuration corresponds, moreover, to the image that many citizens of Rangoon have of their identity. It is a composite identity, resulting from the frequent marriages of male immigrants from Central Burma with females from the Delta area. In this way the cult succeeds in giving expression, although in a more complex and modern way than in the past, to the real state of local ties.

The variability of the criteria determining whether one belongs to a particular. cult, of the relationship between residency and filiation, which has become especially important in the modern context, throws a different light on the religious policy of the Burmese monarchs regarding popular cults. Various hypotheses have been offered about the nature of the religious practices that the *nats* cult supplanted. E. M. Mendelson, while emphasizing the difficulties in trying to establish a general model capable of accounting for the transformation of the *nats*, nevertheless hypothesizes that they are descended from the ancestral spirits of tribal leaders that each community worshipped separately before their unification in the eleventh century.[12] A better idea of the precise nature of the transformations implicit in the institution of the *nats* can be obtained by studying the case of a female spirit, the Buffalo Mare of Pegu, whose cult – probably because it was only recently integrated into the cult of the Thirty-Seven – preserves traces of the ancient practices that it supplanted. One version of the Buffalo Mare ritual, which takes place during the ceremony of the Thirty-Seven, includes the sacrifice of buffaloes, a practice engaged in by the Mons for the marriage of their daughters.

Yet, as I see it, the most important overall benefit to the Burmese kings, in making a *nat* a cultural hero tied to a specific region, is to have territorialized the link of the *nats* to the communities that depend on them. In so doing, the Burmese kings changed the very nature of the ties of identity in these communities: probably quite diverse before their Burmesization, community identity seems now to be defined as a form of local particularism, limited to a defined territory that is part of a national expanse. Moreover, it is embedded and absorbed in the hierarchy of the Buddhist religion, symbolized by an alliance that simultaneously unites and opposes the king to the *nats* through the intermediary of their sisters.

In fact, the essence of this policy has consisted in using the *nats* alone to fuse, on the local level, autochthony and sovereignty. The Thai legend of the Emerald Buddha, by insisting on the act of "forgetting" by the Burmese, seems to point to a specifically Burmese quality. This fusion implies the ambivalence of the cult. Thus the great annual rituals devoted to the *nats*, which take place in the territories they serve, simultaneously contain a regional and national dimension. By the same token, the *nats*, who are supplied with disciplinary power, can turn against either the local population –

through disease, when the local population neglects its *nats* – or the king, when the latter loses his karmic legitimacy. Just as the *nats* serve, on the local level, to uphold simultaneously the principles of autochthony and sovereignty, Thi'dja-Indra occupies an analogously comprehensive position in the symbolic expression of the relationship between the local communities and the monarchy.

Notes

1. This legend is well-known to the mediums. It also told by the Burmese folklorist A. Htin in: *Folk Elements in Burmese Buddhism*, Rangoon, 1975, p. 74. What is interesting about it is the link it establishes between the origin of the cult and the establishment of the Burmese monarchy. However, the actual attribution of the foundation of this cult to Anawratha must be approached with caution: it corresponds to the "necessity" of portraying the first Burmese king to have conquered the Irrawaddy valley as the founder par excellence.
2. See E.M. Mendelson, "L'utilisation du scepticisme religieux dans la Birmanie d'aujourdhui," *Diogenes*, No. 41 (1963); see also H.L. Shorto, "The Dewatau Sotapan: a Mon Prototype of the 37 Nats," in: *B.S.O.A.S.*, Vol. 30, No. 1 (1967), pp. 127-41.
3. This is the case, for instance, with the Lord of the 90,000, the protector of the irrigated district of Kyaukse. Prince Shan, who is ashamed to have to pay homage to Anawratha, prefers to commit suicide, throwing himself into the waters of the Zawgyi river, which is located at the border separating the territories from those of the Burmese king. The latter, infuriated by the disobedience of the prince, rushes to the site of the suicide. Striking the surface of the water with his scepter, he causes the prince to rise to the surface in a position of homage. See also the history of Grandfather Alon that I recounted in *Les Rituels de possession en birmanie*, Paris, 1989.
4. Anawratha was killed on the horns of a wild buffalo which was the incarnation of a spirit whom Anawratha had castrated using Thi'dja's scepter.
5. Quoted in S.J. Tambiah, *World Conqueror and World Renouncer. A Study of Buddhism and Polity against a Historical Background*, Cambridge 1976, p. 73.
6. Ibid., pp. 91-101. See also F.E. Reynolds, "The Holy Emerald Jewel: Some Aspects of Buddhist Symbolism and Political Legitimation in Thailand," in: B.L. Smith (ed.), *Religion and Legitimation of Power in Thailand, Laos, and Burma*, Chambersburg, 1978, pp. 175-93.
7. G. Coedes presents a version of this legend in his "Documents sur l'histoire politique et religieuse du Laos occidental," in: *BEFEO*, Vol. 25 (1925), pp. 287-96. According to this version, which is based on an excerpt from the Thai chronicle called the *Jinkalami*, the Emerald Buddha (of Sinhalese origin), along with the group of texts comprising the canon of Thervadan Buddhism, was given to Anawratha in the eleventh century. On the return voyage, the ship carrying the statue, along with some of the texts, lost its way in a storm and finally reached land not far from Angkor. Later, Anawratha is reported to

have come to Angkor in search of the missing texts but supposedly "forgot" the jewel. The Burmese Chronicle does not mention this incident, asserting instead that these were obtained by the Pagan from the Mon people of Lower Burma, rivals of the Pagan.

8. H. Maspéro, *Le taoïsme et les religions chinoises*, Paris, 1971, pp. 244-53.
9. See B. Formoso in this issue; also Ch. Archaimbault, *Le Sacrifice du buffle à S'iang Khwang (Laos)*, Paris, 1991.
10. As H. Shorto (note 2 above, p. 136) has shown, the double orientation of rituality was also present in another form in the Mon kingdom of Lower Burma.
11. The most celebrated example of this phenomenon is that of the Lord of the Great Mountain and his sister, Golden Face, wife of the Pyu king of Tagaung; but there is also the Lord of the Nine Cities and his sister, Puleyin, wife of Anawratha; and the Great Father of Alon and his sister, the Mother of Running Waters, also a wife of Anawratha. Finally, in the case of serial incarnations, there are brother-sister pairs of minority ethnic origin who follow one after another. Although I am unacquainted with the details of these legends, it is probably fair to assume that they closely follow the above schema.
12. E. M. Mendelson (note 2 above), p. 788.

Tai Cosmology and the Influence of Buddhism

Bernard Formoso

Cosmology of the Non-Buddhist Tai

For the Black, White and Red Tai,[1] the universe is composed of three levels: the heavens, the "flat world," inhabited by man, and the "world beneath the waters," upon which the flat world rests and in which the ophidian genies, the *nguok*, live. These ophidians at times transform themselves into men and devour the heart of young girls. The white Tai imagine that the third level is also peopled by dwarves. The soul is multiple, according to the Tai, and its components become distributed *post mortem* among the two upper levels of the ternary world mentioned above. Indeed, some souls of the deceased migrate to an afterlife in the heavens, others take up residence in the altar of ancestors where they become tutelary household spirits, while the remainder, bound to the body of the deceased, reside in the cemetery.

The heavens in turn are made up of two levels: the world of celestial deities and the abode of the souls of the dead. The world of celestial deities is dominated by the figure of Phi Then Luang ("the divine supreme god") to whom mythology confers the status of universal demiurge. It is he who create and sent the primordial gourds to the earth from which humanity emerged and who, through the intermediary of an emanation, directed mankind, itself incapable of self-rule. In short, according to the schema shared by Tai and Chinese cosmologies, Phi Then Luang made the earth inhabitable and taught mankind the arts of subsistence, through the intermediary of divine heroes. When, tired of being bothered, the supreme god cut the vine or wicker bridge that joined the heavens to the earth, the gods governing mankind became the ancestors of the Tai chiefs, and those who had tilled the lands protected the human communities in their relationship to nature.

The supreme god is surrounded by subordinates who, according to their gender, are called *phi then* ("gods of the heavens") or *mae bao* ("womb mothers"). These deities act in concert to form the souls of the individual about to be born, and in the case of the "womb mothers," to create the model of the bodies in which these souls will become incarnate. Subsequently, by modifying this model, the *mae bao* will be able to sanction good or evil human behavior, while in turn any physical change of the individual caused by accident, illness or aging process would reemerge in its heavenly double. This idea of a womb mother, common to the Chinese and the Tai, maintains, in spite of the rupture of the original tie, a communication between the heavens and the earth through the activity of the shamans who correct the mistakes of their own species.

The abode of the dead is situated at the juncture of the heavens and the earth, along the horizon line. It includes several localities whose number reproduces the differences of rank in Tai society. Thus, among the Black Tai, the souls of common people settle in one village; those of the eminent, whose hereditary duty consists of serving as the chief's auxiliaries, occupy another; those of the chiefs's lineage a third; and finally, the souls of those who assumed the function of chief live in the fourth and final village. The life within these localities reproduces life on earth and magnifies the privileges of the holders of political power. While, in fact, the souls of the common people must work for a living, those of the eminent are excused from all labor, although they are likewise subject to climatic conditions and must, like the former, be reincarnated into minor forms such as caterpillars or moss before disappearing completely. As for the souls of chiefs and members of their lineage, they are much more fortunate, since they have only to wish for something to get it. Furthermore, the climate in their villages is mild and, moreover, they remain in this paradisiacal universe for eternity.

The heavens, as we see, are of fundamental importance to the non-Buddhist Tai. Indeed, from them flows the physical existence, personality, and status of humans, by virtue of a personalized and socially distinctive relationship maintained by each individual with the hierarchical divine beings that people each higher level of the universe.

Below the heavenly deities, there are various supernatural entities that are also designated by the generic term *phi* and which can be divided into two categories. The first includes the tutelary spirits that correspond either to the civilizing heroes from mythic times or to the souls of people who have died normally and joined the altar of the ancestors or the cemetery. These spirits are *a priori* benevolent, but they can punish people who do not respect them or who transgress customs. There are also spirits that are fundamentally malevolent, which are the result of violent deaths, perjurors, or the souls the shaman did not correctly guide toward the villages "to the edge of the horizon" during the funeral rites. Within this second category are also the *phi* who have chosen a particular place (such as a rock, termitary, mountain, forest, tree …) as well as the errant spirits, all the more feared since they cannot be located. While the classification of malevolent spirits varies greatly from one group to another, that of the tutelary spirits is, on the other hand, very stable and defined by virtue of the different levels of the social space. We are indebted to H. Maspéro for having demonstrated that on each different level we are in the presence of a duality similar to that which characterizes the earth gods in ancient China. On the one hand one finds, in fact, a deity that protects the whole of a community living in a specific place. The ancient Chinese call it *she* or *gonshe*, the non-Buddhist Tai call it *phi muang* on the level of the principality (*muang*), *phi ban* on the village level (*ban*), and *phi na* ("spirit of the rice field") on the level of the family. It coexists with another deity, whose protective power is associated exclusively with agnatic filiation. The Chinese call it *sishe*, the Tai call it *lak seua* or *lak muang* when referring to the ruling dynasty, *phi seua* for the other lineages, and *phi hian* for the more restricted level of the household; *phi seua* and *phi hian* are identified with the ancestors either of the lineage or of the domestic unit.

If one considers the most inclusive level, that of the principality, the *lak* and the *phi muang* assume distinct and complementary functions. Through mythological references, each joins the heavens to the earth in its own manner. Hence, the *phi muang*, represented by a tree planted on the outskirts of the community, corresponds to the civilizing hero that the celestial supreme god sent to earth to teach men the arts of subsistence. On the other hand the *lak muang*, represented by a post (*lak*) or a grove of trees, and which is likewise situated outside the living space, symbolizes the bond of filiation uniting the supreme celestial god to the Tai chief, called *tao fa* ("Lord (son) of the heavens").

Another difference between the two deities is seen in the nature of their influence. While the *lak muang* is strictly related to an aristocratic line and the political stratification of its leaders, the jurisdiction of the *phi muang* covers the entire land exploited by the local population. On the other hand, while the chiefs and the *lak muang* associated with them have the role of maintaining social order and civil peace, the *phi muang* is responsible for harmonizing the relationships between nature and man in order to ensure man's health and prosperity. In short, while the *phi muang* gives rise to a public and immutable cult, since as long as the local community exists it worships it no matter the socio-political changes it must confront, the worship of the *lak muang* is private and temporal. Indeed, with each change of dynasty, the new chief knocks down the post symbolizing the authority of his predecessors in order to replace it with a new one, just as in ancient China the new sovereign would neutralize the earth god by walling up the mound of the one he had replaced.

The Cosmology of the Buddhist Tai

Under the influence of Theravada Buddhism, the cosmology of the Tai evolved significantly, first of all, with the emergence of an underworld situated in the bowels of the earth. Similarly, while the *postmortem* fate of the non-Buddhist Tai had been a function of the hereditary status of the deceased, in the Buddhist context this fate became interpreted first and foremost in relation to the moral value of the acts accomplished, in keeping with the doctrine of karma.

Virtue affects status, but, more importantly, virtue establishes status. If, for example, the Laotian or Siamese king places himself at the top of the social hierarchy, it is because he is more advanced than other men in the path that leads to illumination; ideally he is both a *boddhisattva* (a future Buddha) and the *cakkravartin*, that is, he who turns the wheel of Dharmic law in favor of universal harmony. The filial relationship that once tied the king to the celestial supreme god henceforth became replaced by a spiritual tie to the Buddha, and it is this relationship that is believed to legitimize his power.

In the extension of these ideas, the souls of the dead no longer are divided among the heavens and the earth, but henceforth reflect an alternating assignation among the different levels of the universe. Indeed, only the most highly moral people are thought to migrate toward the celestial paradise where their souls live radiantly before being reborn to a higher existence. As for the other deceased, either they descend to expiate their faults in the suffering and overwhelming heat of hell, leaving their descendants with the onus of favoring their rebirth through the accumulation of religious merits; or, in the case of the victims of violent death, they take the form of the *phi* that evolve on earth without hope of reincarnation, as they did in former times, in a typically Buddhist interpretation of their fate, since it is said that their sins are responsible for their premature deaths.

The changes that the Buddhist ideology brought about in terms of the representation of death are found in the more general framework of a redefinition of the relationships to the beyond. Indeed, while men previously had privileged communication with celestial entities, in the Buddhist context the infernal bowels of the earth become the site upon which human imperfection becomes projected, thereby acquiring an importance it never had beforehand. Such a reorientation was reinforced by the phasing out of the *phi then* and the *mae bao* in favor of celestial divinities of Indian origin – the *devata* (*thevada* in Siamese and lao languages) – which Buddhist mythology casts as the auxiliaries or protectors of the works of the Enlightened One.

The *devata* are, as we know, dominated by the distant figure of Brahma and by the more popular one of Indra, their chief, who sits enthroned on the heights of Mount Meru. Like the *phi then*, they are indefinite in number and form a hierarchy. Nevertheless, for the Buddhist Tai, this hierarchy is not a true reflection of that of man, and the belief in the *devata* makes obsolete the ancient idea that the body and the souls of the individual were fashioned by celestial entities and remained under their control for the rest of their lives. Certainly, the fear of celestial mothers is still noticeable in the birth rites of certain Tai Buddhists. But this fear stems from a confusion between the ancient idea of the *mae bao*, that of planetary divinities (*matrka*), originating in Indian astrology, and the properly Buddhist belief relative to the *pho mae kamneut*, that is, the parents from the former life.

For the Buddhist Tai, no longer believing that the *phi then* and the *mae bao* act upon individuals through the intervention of a celestial double, and with the heavens becoming almost inaccessible as a destination for the dead, shamanism, which formerly resolved the problem of the dispersion of the souls of the living and ensured the transfer of some of the souls of the dead to the heavens, will decline, if not disappear, in certain cases, while the search for wayward souls or their reinforcement in the person henceforth will proceed from the collective invocation of the *devata*.

While, to conclude our discussion of the celestial divinities, the belief in Phi Then Luang survives in the Buddhist context, its power on the village level is limited to the mastering of natural elements, and it is no longer invoked except during agrarian rites, when the object is to provoke abundant rainfalls. Buddhism not only profoundly modified the Tai concepts of celestial deities; it also had significant effects on other aspects of their pantheon, as seen in the importance henceforth placed on the subterranean dimension of the universe and reflected in the many functions recognized in Nang Thorani or the *naga*.

Nang Thorani and the Naga

The combination of earth and water upon which the Tai rice growers' subsistence depends will endow the ritual Buddhist context with a very particular nature. Popular Buddhism develops, as we saw, the idea according to which the souls of the majority of dead people migrate underground to expiate their sins. On the other hand, it makes the transfer of merits to ancestors a highly valued act of compassion and faith. In order to concretize this transfer, the Tai will adopt, under the influence of Indian mythology, the very ancient custom in Indochina that consists of pouring alcohol on the earth as an offering to subterranean deities and ancestors, with the nuance that the alcohol becomes replaced by lustral water.

It thus appears that the union between earth and water determines not only the existence of the living, but also the rebirth of the dead inasmuch as it serves as the conductor to virtue in its fight against demonic forces. It is in this role of fecundity and auxiliary to dharma that two figures of Buddhist mythology will become personified as, on the one hand, Dharani (Nang Thorani in Siamese and lao languages) and, on the other, the *naga*, ophidian deities that will merge with the *nguok* from the ancient system of Tai beliefs.

Dharani is one of the feminine divinities personifying the earth in Vedic India. According to legend, Buddha took her as witness to his past merits when Mara contested his authority. Dharani is said to have recalled the time when the Enlightened One poured water over her long hair as a sign of the realization of his meritorious acts. Joining gesture with speech, she allegedly wrung out her hair, producing drops of water that miraculously swelled, becoming transformed into an immense ocean and drowning Mara. It is this mythological episode that the adepts of Theravada Buddhism reenact when they pour water on the earth and take Nang Thorani as witness to the merits addressed to the ancestors. The power to conduct the wicked to hell was, moreover, recognized in this divinity whom the peasants identified with the earth, but who generates anthromorphic representations as well, notably in urban environments. In such cases she is imagined as a young woman, dressed in the manner of princesses of the past and squeezing her long hair, gathered into a single mass, in order to extract the water.

Beside her moral function, Nang Thorani symbolizes the fecundating power of the earth, and her assistance in this respect is invoked by some Buddhist Tai during the main phases of the cycle of rice production. The Laotian farmers, for example, make offerings to her on the occasion of the first workings of the field; they next ask her to help the plants to grow at the time of transplanting; and then they solicit her authorization to proceed in the threshing once the harvest is completed.

Like Nang Thorani, the *naga* reflect material and spiritual concerns. Indeed, they symbolize fertility in a particular guise even as they serve as auxiliaries to Buddha. In this regard, let us recall first of all that Mucalinda, the prince of the *naga*, is said to have protected the Enlightened One from the rain and floods during his meditations in Bodh-gaya by making him a lofty seat out of the coiled rings of his snake body and sheltering him with the hood of his seven heads. On the other hand, through reference to a non-literary tradition known throughout India as well as Southeast Asia, certain Buddhist Tai confer the title of "lord of the *naga*" to another legendary figure, Upagutta. Considered the natural son of Buddha and the fish goddess, Matsa, he is said to have left his retreat at the bottom of the ocean where he lived as a reclusive monk in order to subjugate the Evil One, Mara, who threatened the meritorious works of the famous emperor Asoka.

Similar to Nang Thorani in their roles and the link they create between Buddhism and agrarian cults, the *naga* nonetheless differ from her on several points. First of all, while Nang Thorani personifies the earth, they symbolize fire inasmuch as it is associated with water in a fecundating duality. As in the cosmology of the Chinese or the non-Buddhist Tai, these ophidians live in the underworld upon which the earth rests and which flows out of it in the form of rivers and oceans. On the other hand, while Nang Thorani is a female deity, the Tai conceive of *naga* as masculine beings, since the figure of the *nagini*, popular in Hinduism or Tibetan Buddhism, is not found here.

Theravada Buddhism, moreover, eternalizes an idea already found in the ancient system of Tai beliefs, which casts these ophidians as symbols of virility, the fire they represent being an internal fire, that of male sexuality. Hence the candidates for ordination who have not yet made vows of chastity are qualified as *naga* by the Siamese and Lao, in reference to the legendary episode of Mahavagga according to which a *naga* assumed a human form and had himself ordained bonze at the time of Buddha. His aggressive behavior, however, betrayed his identity and he was defrocked, while as compensation he obtained the promise that candidates for ordination would henceforth be identified with him.

This being so, the cult of the *naga* bears witness to a pronounced ambivalence in their regard. Indeed, in the rites people do not seek their protection as is the case with Nang Thorani, but seek not to awaken their destructive power, or to control their fecundity. Hence, in Laos, during the ritual associated with the first ploughing of the earth, their position is assessed by astrological means. Afterward, the peasants work the fields in the direction of the snake's scales, in order not to wound it and thereby bring on catastrophes. On the other hand, at the time of the rite that calls for rain in the sixth lunisolar month, the Lao peasants explicitly invoke the help of celestial divinities, and during the same rituals they shoot decorated snake-shaped rockets into the sky. The rockets' explosion allegorically signifies the fiery passion of a phallus drawing the vital feminine element of water toward it. Conversely, as harvest time draws near, the same peasants, by means of races in pirogues that here again are *naga*-shaped, enact another coupling that is designed, this time, to attract the waters of the rice fields toward the rivers.

The fear the Tai peasants experience toward the *naga* can be related to the untamed virility these spirits incarnate. This virility is expressed in mythology of Indian origin, but it stems as well from the religious beliefs of the non-Buddhist Tai since, as we mentioned above, the *nguok*, the equivalent of the *naga*, were once thought to have the ability to take on human form in order to seduce and/or devour young girls' hearts. This very ancient theme lives on in residual form, moreover, in Buddhist populations of long standing. R.B. Davis notes that the Khon Muang, the Buddhist Tai in the north of Thailand, distinguish the *naga* from the *ngeuak*, with the latter feared for their ability to devour the souls of humans and the female spirits who inhabit the wood of boats. Elsewhere, the Lao legend that tells of the origins of the rocket festival (*bun bang fai*), associates this institution with the wishes of a king to marry his daughter to the suitor who has made the most powerful rocket (which is to say, implicitly, the one who has proved the most virile). On the outskirts of the competition, one of the sons of the lord of the *naga* was a suitor. Not having been able to get the princess by means of the competition, he tried to seduce her by assuming the form of a squirrel. The plan succeeded to the point that the princess wanted at all costs to possess this squirrel, and a hunter killed it to satisfy her. This provoked the wrath of the lord of the *naga*, and the capital of the kingdom became engulfed in a great cataclysm, while the upheaval of earth of the king's regalia (ring, crown) brought about the creation of ponds and swamps.

Confronted with the ambivalent forces of nature that the *naga* represent to the fullest extent, as is well illustrated by this legend, the Tai developed their cultural project of taming such forces. This project was conceived of as such in the mythology of the ancient Chinese. According to this mythology, the supreme god of the heavens makes the earth liveable and sends celestial heroes there; after a bitter struggle they convert the destructive energy of the master of the earth, the monstrous Gong-gong with horned head and snake's body, into life-giving power. This life-giving power is then held by the earth spirits who are identified with the victorious heroes or the descendants of the vanquished monster.

We have seen that among the Black, White, or Red Tai the role of organizer of the earth and protective divinity of the principality is directly linked to the celestial heroes, while the figure of the monstrous ophidian does not appear here. Nonetheless, Tai mythology bears witness to a stricter influence of the Chinese cosmological model in certain cases, such as in the ancient Indianized kingdom of Luang Phrabang where, as among the ancient Chinese, subjugated ophidian spirits are granted the status of occult protectors of the kingdom along with, it is true, an ensemble of other divinities.

Phi or lak muang?

While the issues of violent death were little affected by the introduction of Buddhism among the spirits that evolve in the invisible dimension of the human world, the changes were much more significant in terms of the protective spirits. The tutelary spirit of the chief's lineage (*lak muang*) and the protective spirit of the community (*phi muang*) will, in fact, most often become fused into a divinity called indiscriminately *phi* or *lak muang*.

It is in the northernmost Tai states on the Indochinese peninsula, more specifically in Luang Phrabang and Chiang Mai, that the old ideas have been the best preserved. In these two cases, the cults of the *lak muang* and the *phi muang* still refer to two distinct bodies of legends. Nonetheless, those relating to the *lak muang* now legitimize the public and unchanging cult of a spirit dissociated from the reigning dynasty. Hence in Luang Phrabang, the *lak muang* is thought either to have been created by two hermits who traced the foundation of the city and assigned the role of protecting it to the *naga*, or to have originally been a sandalwood tree trunk drifting in the water which was fished out by an old woman when she recognized it as a deity. Whatever the legend, however, the *lak muang* no longer personifies, for Luang Phrabang, the filial bond that once linked the chief to the celestial god, and the same is true in Chiang Mai. In the former capital of the kingdom of Lan Na, in fact, the post marking the principality is thought to have been a gift from Indra in order to protect a city that conceived of itself from the outset as a great Buddhist center. From that time on, the *lak muang* served as a palladium for a prominent figure in the Brahmanic pantheon – Indra – whom Buddhism appropriated and who, in the Tai conception, tends to be substituted for the Phi Then Luang, just as the *devata* he directs replaced the *phi then*. As for the *phi muang*, it was subjected to a Buddhist reinterpretation of the ancient schema, including, moreover, a reference to tutelary spirits associated with a population that settled there at a more ancient date. Hence a buffalo is sacrificed each year to the Lawa (Austro-Asiatic) masters of the earth, who are no longer subjugated by the supreme celestial god, but by Buddha.

While in the northernmost kingdoms the difference between *phi* and *lak muang* resisted Buddhist acculturation, in other places the *lak muang*, the post marking the city, personifies the existence of a tutelary spirit identified with the *phi muang*, just as on a lesser level the post marking the village will henceforth serve as a resting place for a collective tutelary spirit.

In this context, the power of the protective spirit is not interpreted through a reference to the deeds of a celestial hero, but refers rather to the action of characters situated on the terrestial plane. In certain, quite rare, cases, there is also mention of fantastic animals. For example, in Meng Long, a former Tai Lü principality of the kingdom of Sip Song Phan Na in Yunnan, a fleeing princess is said to have become miraculously pregnant by drinking water from a footprint left by two Laotian lions. The twin brothers to whom she gave birth then reigned in turn over the locally created principality, while the two lions, whose effigy still sits enthroned in the center of the village, became the tutelary spirits.

Aside from this unusual case, the appropriation of supernatural powers for cultural reasons can sometimes be the result of the workings of bonzes. In the Lao villages on the right and left banks of the Mekong, it is thus very common, following a calamity harshly affecting the community, for the local clergy to set up a *lak ban* (a village post), subduing with psalms the powerful spirit considered to live in the tree or rock chosen as object of the cult. This recognized role of the monks is not, however, restricted to the rural areas. The protective posts of certain great cities in Thailand were erected in the same manner. Khon Kaen, for example, which is the main city of the north- east of the country, was endowed with a *lak muang* in 1956, following the initiative of the chief of the bonzes of the province. He had five basalt stones from an archaeological site that once served as the boundaries of a very ancient temple brought in, and in this way they sheltered the *devata* protecting the pagoda in different directions. One of the stones was placed at the center of Khon Kaen to become the *lak muang*, and the others were placed at the four corners of the city.

In a radically different vein, the *lak muang* is at times identified by the Buddhist Tai with a *phi* created quite simply through the intermediary of a human sacrifice. Indeed, the founding myths of many towns are elaborations on the theme of a violent death that the political power imposes on an individual, or which he imposes on himself. The benevolence of the spirit that issues from this violent end is brought about through the public cult devoted to him from generation to generation. E. Seidenfaden finds these human sacrifices documented in the oral tradition of the Shan of Burma. They are likewise at the center of the founding myths of capitals such as Bangkok, Vientiane, or Luang Phrabang. The sacrificed are often pregnant women because, they say, the spirits engendered by their deaths are particularly dangerous.

Voluntary sacrifices usually manifest themselves after a dream. One of the founding myths of Luang Phrabang mentions in particular a young pregnant woman who was inspired to marry the spirit personified in the post of the city that was to be planted in the earth and who, decked out in red flowers, threw herself into the hole to share the fate of her husband. As for involuntary sacrifices, they are most often designated through divination. For example, the oral tradition of the ancient *muang* of Roi Et, in the north-east of Thailand, traces the institution of the protective post of the principality to a soothsayer's choice of two men from a list of those subject to forced labor. On the order of the nobleman who had just founded the city, the two men were impaled by means of a post that was to materialize their power, a post taken from a "candle tree" (*hopea odorata*), whose abundant secretions of resin already in themselves manifest a supernatural presence.

One can't conclude this panorama of themes dominating the foundation myths of the Buddhist Tai principalities without mentioning the most recurrent theme among them, which conceives of the *muang* tutelary spirit as a human, identified with the local history and whose power is revealed during his lifetime through the acquisition of a higher status. This character is at times a hero of renown in the region, whose protective power is appropriated by many localities at the same time. Let us take, for example, the ancient principality of Nong Bua Lamphu in the current province of Udon (north-east of Thailand). Here they make tutelary deities out of Pha Daeng and Nang Hai, two of the principal actors of the creation myth of *bun bang fai*, the rocket festival, which is the most important rain-invocation ritual celebrated by the Lao. Like the inhabitants of many other localities of the North-East, the inhabitants of the Nong Bua Lamphu justify the cult they devote to pseudo-historic celebrities by asserting that they were born there. These same inhabitants likewise appropriated another regional hero in the figure of Phu Lup. Phu Lup is said to have been an officer in the army of the Vientiane king, Chao Anu (1805-1827), who very early on demonstrated supernatural powers. Chao Anu dismissed him, seeing in him a *phi phop*, which is to say a particularly dangerous devourer of souls. After this slight, Phu Lup took refuge in a forest today adjoining a district near the Nong Bua Lamphu. There he confirmed his reputation as *phi phop* even further by causing the death of his wife, his daughters, and other women. The *devata* reacted by causing an earthquake that buried Phu Lup. After his death, the inhabitants of Nong Bua Lamphu, and especially men seeking virility, tamed his fearful power by making him *phi muang* beside Pha Daeng and Nang Hai.

The guardian spirits associated with the preceding cases are all in all less numerous in comparison to others derived from people more closely tied to the creation of a city, a village, or even a monastic community. In Thailand, as in Laos, many are the princes, generals or great monks who were identified after their deaths as the tutelary spirit of the collectivity they founded and successfully ran; the same phenomenon recurs frequently in rural villages. We should note that the spirits formed in this way are often considered communal ancestors. The Lao of the north-east of Thailand thus qualify the *phi-lak muang* as *chao pho* ("lord-father") to indicate their ancendancy over human activity and a more or less extensive ensemble of secondary protective deities. As for village tutelary spirits, they are called, in the same sense, *ta pu ban*, that is, "maternal or paternal village grandfather."

In the few cases of *muang* in which it is possible to reconstruct the process of ancestralization, we note that it operates in two time periods. The lord first imposes on his subjects the idea that the principality he has founded is protected on the occult level by his *pho mae kamneut*, his father and mother from a former life, using the popular Buddhist beliefs on the subject to his advantage. Then, at a later point corresponding to his death, he is identified with his karmic parents.

It is certainly very interesting to examine what happens to the public worship of such deities during a change of command. Does the new sovereign continue the worship of his predecessors or does he substitute an analogous cult based on his own *pho mae kamneut*? Based on the study undertaken by Ch. Archaimbault (1959) on the Lao kingdoms of Luang Phrabang and Xieng Khuang, it would appear that the idea of plurality is preferable to substitution and that the official cult always preserves a preeminent place in the dynasty that founded the principality or kingdom. In Luang Phrabang, the *phi muang* is made up of a group of spirits dominated by the figure of the Phu Nieu Nia Nieu, the founding celestial heroes, who were later assimilated into the *devata*. At the heart of this assembly one finds the monarchs who were thought to be the descendants of Then Luang, through reference to the ancient Tai mythology. One of them is none other than Suvanna Khampong, the grandfather of Fa Ngum who condemned his grandson to exile in 1353 to prevent him from dethroning him. Fa Ngum was himself deified after his death, like his son, Sam Sen Tai, who overthrew him in 1373. As for Xieng Khuang, where the *lak* and *phi muang* are confused, more than thirty princes and monarchs are honored there simultaneously as protective ancestors. In both cases, the distribution of offerings and other aspects of the rites express a hierarchy that favors precedence, status, and fame, while placing the deified monarch above the chthonian spirits and subjugated ophidians.

The process of ancestralization we have just examined is quite similar to the comparable concept of the *lak muang* among the non-Buddhist Tai, since in both cases the power of the protective spirit depends on a filial relationship. However, there is a major difference on the level of the ideas underlying each form of worship. Except for the special case in Luang Phrabang between the sixteenth and seventeenth centuries, the lord is no longer considered to rule because he is of divine ancestry, but the fact that he governs attests to virtuous ancestors, capable of patronizing the kingdom. In other words, the *lak muang* does not legitimize the power of the lord, it prolongs it. It is no longer the mark of an exclusive filial relationship with the supreme celestial god, but merely expresses a fate and a superior capacity that can be shared with others (from which comes perhaps the facility to accumulate tutelary spirits in certain kingdoms or principalities). Similarly, the *lak muang* is no longer traced back to the feats of a divine hero, but to those of an historical or pseudo-historical personage. In short, let us remember that it no longer reflects a private and temporal cult, but a public and immutable one.

While the *phi* and *lak muang* merged under the influence of Buddhism to the point that one can describe them as *phi-lak muang*, and while the beliefs concerning their origins have become modified and diversified, the great universal religion did not, however, weaken popular faith in the protective powers that were once recognized in the tutelary spirits of the principalities or villages, and this is what allowed them to maintain a strict link between these spirits and the holders of political power. Very indicative of the importance they still hold is the fact that Bangkok today has two *phi-lak muang*, placed side by side, because the great king Mongkut (1851-1868), though known for his modern spirit and Buddhist faith, learned from a diviner that the one instituted by his grandfather seventy years earlier did not correspond to his horoscope. Let us add that the practice continues in Thailand of instituting *phi-lak muang* in provincial towns that were not endowed with them beforehand. This is often at the initiative of the governors or district chiefs who hope in this way to place their administrations under favorable auspices or to exorcise a series of calamities. They then call upon the monks to transform the untamed spirits into a positive force.

The importance still granted to the cult of tutelary spirits by the governors and the ensemble of the population is explained by the widely held conviction of their omnipotence. They strengthen the power of the authorites first of all by punishing the crimes of trouble-makers and traitors. On these grounds, the king of Thailand, as did his Laotian counterpart, invites them to follow the periodic ceremony during the course of which all the civil servants of the kingdom renew their faith in him. They likewise protect the collectivity from any external threats, be it from malevolent spirits or human aggressors. One gets an idea of the faith they inspire through a popular saying in the north of Thailand, according to which they can transform "assailants into peaceful merchants." If they cease to respond to popular appeal in the area of security, then the very fate of the collectivity is severely threatened. The event related by H. G. Quaritch Wales, based on sources from Burma and tied to the dissolution of the kingdom of Ayuthaya in 1767, is very indicative of this Tai belief. Having failed in all his attempts to break the surrounding of his capital by the Burmese army, the king of Siam ordered that all the inhabitants of Ayuthaya make appropriate offerings to the tutelary spirit of the city, who from ancient times was thought to reside in the barrel of a large cannon. This cannon was then hoisted with great ceremony onto the top of the northernmost surrounding wall, across from the enemy camp. It was loaded with ample ammunition, but the lighting of the fuse failed several times. The officers unloaded it, and learned with terror that the powder had been changed into water. They then understood that their situation was hopeless.

Directly involved in the social order and in the defense of the group when confronted by an adversary, guardian spirits are likewise capable of salutary action against the forces of nature and can fend off epidemics or intervene favorably in climatic equilibrium by making rains come in times of drought, or drying up flooded areas. In short, they have the reputation of having as much influence over collective fate as over that of the individual, and are constantly solicited by individuals who thank them with gifts of money or food in return for an answered prayer (healing of a sick person, prosperity regained, successful participation in a competition).

It goes without saying that the different facets of their power vary in importance according to the social scale and context. On the level of the kingdom, the official cult seeks political integrity and prosperity set forth on a large scale. On the village level, on the other hand, agricultural preoccupations take precedence and the collective rites devoted to them correspond to the seasonal changes that govern the productive activity of the peasants.

The punishment of traitors, mentioned earlier, recalls the fundamental ambivalence of these deities, and the history of the most powerful tutelary spirits is marked with people who have died for having neglected or defied them. Placating them implies in fact that people show them respect by using certain forms of salutation, make offerings to them, respect the promises or oaths made in their presence, refrain from spoiling the area of their sanctuary and, lastly, keep them abreast of all the important matters concerning the collectivity or the families that comprise it. As regards this final mark of deference, H. G. Quaritch Wales reports that, up until the year 1910, the king of Siam never failed to send an invitation to the guardian spirit of Bangkok, requesting that he honor with his presence the state ceremonies that were being organized. In certain rural villages, it is still common practice to inform these spirits of the celebration of important events such as births, marriages, deaths, or even to ask them to accept newcomers and protect villagers absent for long periods of time.

We have until now dissociated the village guardian spirits from their counterparts on the higher administrative echelons. Nevertheless, in the Tai Buddhist system of representations, like that of the ancient Chinese, the ensemble of spirits forms a hierarchy that reproduces the political hierarchy of the country on a supernatural plane. Hence, although such a pyramidal structure is never perfectly reflected in rituals, the spirits of the villages are suboordinate to those of the district, themselves dominated by the tutelary spirits of the province (formerly the principality), whose power is nonetheless inferior to that of the guardian deities of the kingdom. One of the most poignant examples of this hierarchy is found in Xieng Khuang. In fact, in this ancient Lao kingdom, the sanctuary of the *phi muang* once included twelve altars to the image of Louang Phrabang. According to Ch. Archaimbault, eleven of these altars, smaller than the twelfth, were in fact devoted to the village protective spirits, who served as "lower" chiefs to the kingdom's supreme tutelary spirit.

Let us note, to complete this rapid examination of the occult patronage of Buddhist collectivities, that the various themes defining the origin and power of protective spirits become willingly superimposed on the local level. Thus to the idea of human sacrifice is often added that of the submission of a regional *phi* by the monks or the transformation of the community's founding hero into a tutelary ancestor. The former principality of Roi Et, already mentioned above, well illustrates this phenomenon. The *lak muang* there today includes three active forces, since to the magical properties of the "candle" tree and the souls of the two men buried beneath the post derived from this tree, was later added the spirit of the prince who founded the *muang*. Let us go back to the case of Nong Bua Lamphu where, aside from the tamed ogre Phu Lup and the legendary couple Nang Hai/Pha Daeng, people worship two cousins who founded the principality in 1766, following the disgrace of one of them, Pha Va, who had been minister of the king Ong Bun of Vientiane. Many other examples could be quoted to illustrate a tendency toward a proliferation of tutelary deities.

While a lack of efficacy among the preexisting spirits can at times reactivate this tendency, this is far from the case most of the time, and to explain the strong recurrence of this phenomenon one might do better to speak of a mixture of fear and eclecticism, with the collectivity employing every means at her disposal in the face of adversaries deemed all-powerful. This frame of mind, furthermore, is found in a very syncretic practice of Buddhism and in the concern the Tai have always had to turn to their own advantage the cult of earth spirits once belonging to people they have conquered.

* * *

I have attempted here to outline the influences that Indianization had on the Tai cosmology and on their conception of earth deities. As we have seen, Buddhism imposed a new way of interpreting fate, which resulted in a redefinition of divine entities, their hierarchy, and their relationships to humanity. The status of the individual was henceforth interpreted in relation to the moral value of his past deeds and no longer on the basis of a differentiated descent supposedly initiated by the deities. The heavens toward which most of the religious practices of the non Buddhist Tai were directed lost importance in favor of the earth and subterranean world. And even if, according to popular Buddhism, the future Buddha sojourns in the higher level of celestial paradise, it is a spiritual link, like that between master and disciple, and not a geneological relationship, between ancestors and descendants, that ties the supreme divine entity to the sovereign.

These changes influenced the ancient Tai belief system by means of the classic phenomena of fusion and substitution. Hence, the convergent symbolism of the *nguok* and the *naga* favored their amalgamation (even if this was only partially the case in certain regions) at the same time that it increased the importance conferred on ophidian spirits. For their part the *devata* became substituted for the *phi then*, the former celestial divinities, just as Indra or Buddha took the place of Phi Then Luang as supreme deity, and each of these permutations corresponds to significant changes in the Tai belief system. Hence, the abandonment of the relationship of procreation according to which individuals or social groups derived from a celestial intervention greatly favored the amalgamation of *phi* and *lak muang*.

There was not, however, any sharp break with the former religious concepts, but rather a reciprocal and progressive adaptation, with Buddhist dogma evolving into the popular religion, in correspondence with the material preoccupations of the peasants, while the former concepts became reinterpreted in conformity with the ideology of the Enlightened One. This process of reciprocal integration is still in progress and, in the absence of uniformity, contributes to the great variety of earth divinities to which the Tai devote cults. Many of these deities coexist all the better as they take on complementary roles. For example, the flamboyant and barely tamed virility of the *naga* contrasts with the wise Nang Thorani, vehicle of the merits transferred to the dead and mistress of their destiny, while these two deities in turn are distinguished from the *phi/lak muang* by the fact that they do not represent a particular community and have no political dimension. The *phi* and *lak*, whatever the level on which they are worshipped (whether by family, village, principality, kingdom) manifest, in fact, the property of being tied in an exclusive way to a localized social group. Defined as tutelary ancestors or occult allies of the sovereign, they watch over the security and the prosperity of the group and, in this way, are one of its main identifying characteristics.

Notes

1. The term *t'ai* refers to a family of ethnic languages to be found between the South of China and the various countries of the Indochinese peninsula. The Tai who populate Thailand and Laos are among the best-known belonging to this family. The Black, White, and Red Tai – so called because of the color of the traditional dress preferred by their women – for that matter live in the mountainous regions of North Vietnam.

The author has not systematically cited all the works upon which he has based his arguments, but they may be found in the following bibliography:

Archaimbault, Ch., "La naissance du monde selon les traditions lao: le mythe de Khan Bulom," in: *Sources orientales I, la naissance du monde*, Paris, 1959, pp. 385-414.

Idem, "La fête du T'ai à S'ieng Khwang (Laos), contribution à l'étude du Ti K'i," in: *Artibus Asiae*, Vol. 24 (1961), pp. 187-200.
Idem, "La fête du T'ai à Luang Phrabang," in: ibid., Supplement XXIII, Vol. 1 (1966), pp. 5-47.
Idem, "Le liang du hô devata luang à Luang Phrabang, in: *Bulletin de la Société des Etudes Indochinoises*, Vol. 46, No. 2 (1971), pp. 217-86.
Bonifacy, A.L.M., "Les rites de mort chez les Tho," in: *Revue Indochinoise*, No. 6 (March 1904), pp. 361-65.
Chavannes, E., "Le dieu du sol dans la Chine antique," in: *Le T'ai Chan. essai de monographie d'un culte chinois*, Paris, 1910, pp. 437-527.
Condominas, G., "Phiban Cults," in: W. Skinner and A.T. Kirsch (eds.), *Change and Persistence in Thai Society*, Ithaca, 1975, pp. 252-73.
Davis, R., *Muang Metaphysics. A Study of Northern Thai Myth and Ritual*, Bangkok, 1984.
Duroselle, Ch., "Upagutta et Mara," in: *BEFEO*, Vol. 4, No. 1/2 (1904), pp. 414-28.
Finot, L., "Recherches sur la littérature laotienne," in: ibid., Vol. 17 (1917), pp. 149-64.
Formoso, B., "Alliance et séniorité, le as des Laos du nord-est de la Thailande," in: *L'Homme*, No. 115 (1990), pp. 71-97.
Idem, "Le bun pha We:t des lao du nord-est de la Thailande," in: *BEFEO*, Vol. 79, No. 2 (1992), pp. 238-60.
Lafont, P.H., "Notes sur les familles patronymiques thaïes noires de S'on-La et de Nghia-Lo," in: *Anthropos*, No. 50 (1955), pp. 797-807.
Levy, P. "Le sacrifice du buffle et la prédiction du temps à Vientiane," in: R. Berval (ed.), *Présence du royaume lao, France-Asie*, No. 118/20 (1956), pp. 846-56.
Lunet de la Jonquère (ed.), *Ethnographie du Laos septentrional*, Paris, 1906.
Maspéro, H., *Le Taoïsme et les religions chinoises*, Paris (1950), 1971.
Mus, P., "Les cultes indiens et indigènes au Champa," in: *BEFEO*, Vol. 33, No. 1 (1933), pp. 367-410.
Idem, *Barabudur*, New York (1935), 1978.
Nimnanhaeminda, K., "The Lawa Guardian Spirits of Chiang Mai," in: *Journal of the Siam Soiety*, Vol. 55, No. 2 (1967), pp. 185-226.
Pottier, R., *Le système de santé lao et ses possibilités de développement*, Thèse d'Etat, University René Descartes, Paris, 1979.
Idem, "Mythes et folklores des peuples thaïs," in: *Mythes et croyances du monde entier*, Vol. 4, Paris, 1985, pp. 235-347.
Przyluski, J., *La Légende de l'empereur Açoka dans les textes indiens et chinois*, Paris, 1923.
Quaritch-Wales, H.G., *Siamese State Ceremonies*, London, 1931.
Rajadhon, (Phya) Anuman, "The Phi," in: *Journal of the Siam Society*, Vol. 41 (1954), pp. 153-78.
Rhys-David, T.W., and Oldenberg, H., *Mahâvaggo*, Oxford, 1884.
Robert, R., *Notes sur les Tay Dèng de Lang Chanh* (Mémoire, No.1, I.I.E.H.), Hanoi, 1941.
Seidenfaden, E., *The Thai Peoples*, Bangkok, 1958.
Silvestre, Capitaine, "Les Thais Blancs de Phong-Tho," in: *BEFEO*, Vol. 18, No. 4 (1918), pp. 1-56.
Tambiah, S.J., *Buddhism and the Spirit Cults in North-East Thailand*, Cambridge, 1970.

Yan Vliet, J., "Description of the Kingdom of Siam," in: *Journal of the Siam Soiety*, 7/1910, pp. 1-108 (1st ed. 1638).
Wijeywardene, G., "The Still Point and the Turning World: Towards the Structure of Northern Thai Religion," in: *Mankind*, 7/1970, pp. 247-55.
Idem, *Place and Emotion in Northern Thai Ritual Behaviour*, Bangkok, 1986.
Zago, M., *Rites et cérémonies en milieu bouddhiste lao*, Rome, 1972.

Ties of Blood
and Earth in Japan

Laurence Caillet

Inhabitants of a land that their ancient myths proclaimed to be the creation of divinities, the Japanese have peopled their archipelago with numerous earth gods: giants trees, simple pebbles concealed either in an oratory, a corner of a garden or deep inside a thicket; crossroads stoneposts, steles in the middle of a plot or next to a rice field, tombstones, and rocks that are worshipped on home altars. The imposing presence of these divine proprietors of the provinces and of sites that were once urban settlements, villages, or private residences is still visible in the tall buildings of Tokyo and Osaka. These protean spirits, found on roof tops in the form of stone foxes or redwood porticos, bear witness, even in the heart of the city, to a latent belief: the forces of the earth are still at work in the world, keeping watch over human activities. Although there are very few people left who believe, as the ancients stories tell, that the citizens of Japan are descendants of the gods of the earth and sky, there nevertheless remain many who accept the notion that a single telluric energy inhabits the world of the living, the dead, things, and the gods.

Analyzing ancient tales and contemporary practices, we will try here to follow how an intrinsic confusion in the very conception of the Japanese earth god – a confusion between territoriality and the fertility of the soil – gave rise to a constant imbrication between ties of blood and earth that endures until today. Described variously as territorial gods, ancestors who cleared the land, purified forms of ancestors, evil spirits, or as gods of agriculture and other chthonic forces, these local gods have become part of a single community of men and earth that has certainly strengthened feelings of local identity.

The Mythology of the Eighth Century

Looking over the list of gods who qualified as earth gods in the ancient texts[1] of the indigenous Shinto religion, we can immediately see that there existed four distinct conceptions of these supernatural entities. They are either chthonic gods who oppose the celestial gods, occupants of the national territory prior to the establishment of the power of the celestial gods on earth; gods who begat the soil, or finally certain gods of the ocean.

These myths, recast for current taste by premodern and modern Shinto exegesis, call these earth gods *chijin* and describe them as comprising the five direct ascendants of the first human emperor, Jinmu, who is said to have taken the throne in 660 B.C. As earth gods, they are in opposition to the *tenjin*, or celestial gods; in other words, to the first seven generations of gods who embody the logical and physical processes that created the world. These imperial ancestors, however, who like their descendants succeeded in a direct line as rulers of the country from the creation of the world (this, at least, was what was taught in Japanese schools until 1945), are also called "celestial gods." Popular knowledge in fact rejects the differentiation that the Sino-Japanese terms *tenjin* and *chijin* introduced into the chronology of the world's creation. It is more interested in the confrontation between *kuni tsu gami* ("gods of the country" [of the archipelago and its provinces]) and the *ama tsu gami* ("the celestial gods").[2]

Part of a dualistic pantheon, these territorial gods contrast with the celestial divinities who are cast as the principal progenitors and legitimate sovereigns of the islands. Nevertheless, according to Japanese cosmogony, some of the earth gods were born in the heavens. These divinities, as representatives of the lower world in the empyrean, thus appear to be able to maintain special ties – of protection and ancestrality – with gods who are more authentically terrestrial. As for the latter, they seem to arise out of the earth itself, although on occasion they are capable of begetting islands in the manner of the celestial gods, or at least building and consolidating them. The local gods, incarnating earthly vitality and untamed nature, thus governed the Japanese lands before the arrival of the celestial powers.

The pacification of the country by the legitimate celestial gods is described as taking place in various ways: through war or marriage with the earth gods, or by the establishment of a ritual alliance with them; and none of these modes of submission excludes the other. In the absence of restrictive rules of succession (all descendants of the agnatic line for five generations or more could be a candidate for office), the support of an influential terrestrial father-in-law often proved to be decisive in quarrels between celestial cousins. Moreover, the ritual alliance, whose form was a cult that the living celestial sovereigns offered to their chthonic ancestors forced into the other world, transformed these rivals not into affines but ancestors: adopted as sons-in-law, the celestial gods inherited the terrestrial sovereigns who preceded them. In any case, and as was emphasized by the Japanese scholars of the premodern nationalist school known as "National Studies," local and celestial gods were related. Beginning in Antiquity, the increase in alliances of marriage between celestial and local gods had "obligatorily" established ties of consanguinity between the two categories of gods. What's more, as gods of the islands begotten by the cosmogonic gods of the heavens, the local gods were in some sense the descendants of the celestial gods, which did not prevent some of them from passing themselves off as *ubusuna-gami*, "progenitor gods of the earth," as well.

In any case, the local gods are generally considered to be the original proprietors of the earth. And because territorial appropriation and cultural development are intertwined here, their pacification justifies the clearing of the land and the establishment of human communities. The ancient myths tell of how the gods were confined to uncultivated regions, either in the mountains above water sources or even in the other world; and of how some of them – snakes, dragons, or fish – accepted or decided to remain in areas hostile to man as long as they were worshipped in an appropriate manner. Once the earth gods were subdued, the trees and rocks ceased to drone like flies and to complain by keeping their voices constantly raised. Henceforth, only the sovereign's word would be heard above the silence – a word embodied in a form of ritual speech perfectly effective in matters of governance. The ancient tales also tell of how one of these gods, who had an apelike appearance, remained with the sovereign in order to marry the celestial ancestor of a group of ape-keeping acrobats who are presented as the distant founders of the No theater; as a result, the descendants of some of the local gods, talented actors who can imitate men, the dead, and the gods, are still walking the earth.[3]

Genealogy and Hierarchy

The ancient genealogical texts testify to the fact that the Japanese aristocracy liked to claim for itself a more or less divine origin: in a court where status was assessed simultaneously in terms of wealth and antiquity, the hierarchy of the nobility was reflected in one's proximity to the imperial line, which was the most celestial of all. However, because the vagaries of fortune sometimes resulted in the violation of the rule of lines of celestial origin over those of local provenance, genealogical tables often had to be revised in order to maintain the veracity of the principle on which the State was founded. Also, for a long time, aristocrats demanded that promotion within the bureaucracy be tied to one's birth rank.[4]

It should be emphasized here that although the ancient texts make use of the word *kuni*, which designates a territory and its borders; and of the word *ubusuna*, which expresses the vitality of the processes associated with begetting; and of the Sino-Japanese lexeme *chi*, which means earth, the Japanese acceptation of this same character, *tsuchi*, does not seem to be commonly used in this context. This is probably because *tsuchi*, the only one of these terms – along with *kuni* – that is immediately understandable to all Japanese speakers, has a very negative connotation. For instance, the earth taboo, the forbidding of walking on the ground during certain rituals, is called "standing apart from *tsuchi*." Metaphorically, the color of earth stands for ugliness and coarseness. Finally, lower-ranking bureaucrats, who do not have the right to enter the inner sanctum of the Royal Palace, are called "earthen," *tsuchi*. The earth gods, even though lower ranking than the celestial spirits, are themselves marked by a profound ambivalence. Associated with the other world, they share the ambiguous position of the dead, seen both as protective and threatening.

Contemporary Names for the Earth Gods

Although one almost never meets with the term "local god," both the Japanese countryside and the streets of its cities are peopled with earth gods. Called "earth gods" (*chijin, chi no kami*, or *ji-gami*), "proprietary gods of the soil" (*jinushi-gami*), or even "the god of the inhabited area" (*yashiki-gami*), they are of a complex nature. The multiple glosses associated with the names of these minor gods – often no more than a pebble inside an oratory or an indentation on a piece of white paper – bear witness to this complexity. In some cases their names are linked to other, more generic terms, such as *uchi-gami* (house god), *uji-gami* (lineage god), *ubusuna-gami* (birthplace god), *wakamiya* (unfortunate dead), *yama no kami* (mountain god), and others. In still other cases they conceal more individuated divinities, who are not characterized as earth gods and are instead associated with regional sanctuaries well known throughout the country: Inari, Gion, Kumano, Tenno, Hakusan, Atago, Akiba, Hachiman, etc. Some of these famous names, however, are in reality toponyms, i.e. contemporary names for renowned sanctuaries at which a multiplicity of divinities, along with their innumerable variants (all of which are listed in the great texts of Buddhism and Shintoism), are worshipped.

In brief, the name of one god always conceals other gods. As indispensable as the earth gods as such are, almost any divinity, or group of divinities, can fill their role. Also, all the gods, whether of earth or not, have a local character because they are all currently designated by their place of residence. As a result, Inari and Hachiman, the most venerated of all Japan's gods, are often worshipped as earth gods, because the number of sanctuaries, small and large, dedicated to their memory numbers in the hundreds of thousands. Everyone knows that they are respectively the god of rice or commerce and the god of war. Some have been told that Hachiman is in reality Ojin, the fifteenth emperor of the archipelago. But almost no one knows that other gods are concealed behind their names. For instance, the scholarly glosses of Shintoism notably identify Inari with the goddess of food whose corpse, according to the ancient myths, is the source of cultivated plants and domesticated animals. The Buddhist monks, on the other hand, see in her the Japanese form of Dakini, a goddess of Indian origin: she is the creature who, knowing the death of individuals six months in advance, waits for the day of their death in order to devour their hearts. First she was converted to Buddhism; then, as she was represented as riding on a fox, the Japanese associated her with Inari, a god whose messenger is a fox. As for Hachiman, he includes not only Ojin but Ojin's mother, the Empress Jingu, as well as a great anonymous goddess for whom the emperor Chuai, Ojin's father, is sometimes substituted.

A single earth god can be worshipped by all the houses of a village, independent of the local or ancestral connotation of the word used to designate it. However, only the ancestral houses themselves are permitted to celebrate their own earth god, with one exception: when the divinity is worshipped collectively by its *dozoku* (i.e. a "hierarchical grouping of related houses"). Some Japanese ethnologists, and in particular the founder of Japanese ethnology, K. Yanagita, believe that the local gods, whom the most ancient texts identified as ancestral in nature, were honored by the ancestral homes of the *dozoku* alone. When, over time, it became more and more difficult to maintain the integrity of hierarchies based on family age, first all the houses composing these hierarchically grouped entities and, later, literally all the inhabitants of the local communities, began to worship this divinity. Thus, under the influence of local conditions, the earth god progressively lost its ancestral quality.[5] However, this historicist conception of the evolution of the earth gods must be rejected because, although the cult of the earth gods exists throughout Japan, the *dozoku* are only found in the eastern provinces of the archipelago. Thus the imbrication of ties of blood and earth would seem to be not a historical development but present from the beginning.

The Earth God as Ancestral Divinity

There are in Japan many traditions that identify the earth god with the deified form of either the founding ancestor of a group of related houses or village, or even with the ancestor who acquired the land on which the ancestral home was originally built. In any case, the Japanese language always calls these spirits "land-clearer ancestors." At the same time, there are other local interpretations that say that the earth god is the totality of all the deceased ancestors of a single lineage. Nevertheless, the term *uji-gami*, lineage god, is not in all cases linked to the attribution of an ancestral nature to this local divinity. Indeed this ancestral quality of the earth god is sometimes utterly denied. In other cases, the ancestral characteristic is revealed to its descendants only much later, by means of an oracle. For instance, when a particular family, neighborhood or village is hit with a series of misfortunes, it is often necessary to turn to a medium in order to discover the cause. Through the medium it is then learned that the local god that has been worshipped for such a long time under the name of "lineage god" is in fact, as his name indicates, an ancestor.

On the other hand, the fact that an ancestral divinity is called, for example, Inari, like the renowned rice god whose home is in the town of Fushimi Inari, to the south of Kyoto, does not necessarily imply a desire to establish ties of filiation with this famous god. Rather, it can be quite reasonably asserted that the local Inari possesses an ancestral nature without thereby including Inari of Fushimi among its ancestors; and yet at the same time the two entities called Inari need not be considered as different. The divine ancestors called Inari are in fact thought of as local embodiments of the original Inari, but the existence and function of these local gods precede their association with the rice god. Instead, their association with him provides them with an additional quality.

The designation of an ancestral god as an earth god rarely gives rise to a real genealogical working-out, establishing the exact relation between a god and its name. As an example of this, let us take a look at an extreme case, i.e., that of five groups of hierarchically arranged houses, located in the county of Yamanashi (Kita Koma canton, Sudama district), all of whom bear the famous last name Fujiwara, a family that once played a leading role at the Heian Court.[6] These five *dozoku*, who make a vague claim of being descendants of the great Fujiwaras, gather to worship a large round stone, called Onogoro, which is kept inside a small chapel constructed of rocks and located in the middle of a field belonging to the ancestral house of the one among them whom they consider the eldest. The name Onogoro is written with the help of an ideogram for the word "ax," which evokes the clearing of land, and with the characters signifying "fifth son." Onogoro is supposed to be the first name of an ancestor who was a land-clearer peasant, which seems to conflict with the idea of his aristocratic heritage. However, Onogoro is also the name of the very first Japanese island, which "took solid form by itself" after the sea had been churned up by the progenitor deities. However, the written form adopted by the families conceals the homophony that links the local phenomenon to the originary island. These farmers make reference to paragons of courtly refinement, to ancient cosmology and modern means of land clearing, without establishing any kind of link among the different origins.

The Earth God and Unfortunate Death

The earth gods who let their anger be known by oracle are not always related to those whom they threaten. Indeed, the earth gods often appear as manifestations of "bad deaths," beings deceased in acts of violence, to whom no cult was offered and whose unquenched passion for life attaches them too strongly to this world. Sometimes they are ancestors who died in tragic circumstances and who are simply dissatisfied with the way their descendants are worshipping them. Most often, however, they are warriors, members of the famous Heike clan of the eleventh and twelfth centuries that was wiped out by the Minamotos. In the twelfth century, fugitive Heikes were cut down throughout the Japanese provinces, tricked by their hosts of an evening or murdered in cowardly fashion by the pursuing Minamotos. There are also women of long ago, high aristocrats, who died in distant provinces. Now, centuries later, these "bad deaths," these evil spirits, reappear, recounting their torments through the intermediary of an exorcist or a medium who has been consulted by people interested in knowing the causes of their own life difficulties.

Independent of whether real ties of filiation exist, all these dead are treated as family members. The spirits, as a result of the periodic offerings they receive, gradually lose their savage nature to become tutelary gods, and in fact some of them are officially adopted by communities of worshippers. The leader of this community then has the monks in the local monastery make a funerary slab, which he buries next to the earth god's chapel oratory. Nevertheless, all these spirits retain an inner violence – much greater, it is said, than that of other divinities – which incites them to inflict punishments on those who either neglect their ritual duties or provide the god with unsuitable offerings. These gods, called *araburu-gami* ("the dreadful god"), *ubusuna Kojin* ("Kojin who begets the soil"), or *heso no o Kojin* ("Kojin of the Navel"), sometimes demand that all who have been born on the lands ruled by him return home to celebrate the rituals of the god of their birthplace. They share the strength and anger of *Fudo myoo*, the king of Fudo wisdom, known as the Immobile One (Sanskrit *Acalanatha*). Also known as *wakamiya* ("young masters"), these gods also manifest the irritability of the recently deceased.

These savage gods reveal the importance of places of birth and death much more clearly than do the gods normally inserted into ancestral lineages. Indeed their importance is so great that no one would dare move an earth god, irrespective of whether it possessed an ancestral nature or not. In fact, in times past, many epidemics, fires, and other catastrophes were set off by gods who had been moved in this way; and the terrors continued until the gods were returned to their place of origin. Prudence thus demands that humans wait until an oracle has clearly expressed the necessity of moving them to a new place of residence.

Everyone knows that the earth gods are jealous by nature and not to be trusted. For instance, in a certain family group, it was customary that only the heads of household of the ancestral house dedicated a cult to the earth god Kojin; but then Kojin demanded that all the houses of the area participate in his worship. It was then decided that the organizing of Kojin's annual celebration would fall on each house in turn. Yet at the same time, the soil god only allowed the members of the eldest house to cut the wood in the forest from which his sanctuary was to be constructed. Any transgression on the part of the younger families would provoke his anger. Thus this is a god capable of being unjust. Perhaps his actions bear witness to the fact that the most reliable relations combine ties of blood and earth simultaneously.

Earth Gods and the Life Cycle

According to widely held beliefs, the final commemoration of the death of a deceased coincides with this deceased's reaching the status of a god. Thirty-three, fifty, or even a hundred years after death, the deceased finally escapes the jurisdiction of the funerary religion, Buddhism, to become *kami*, a god of the Shinto religion, or at least to merge with a divine entity who is simultaneously ancestral and tutelary. In some cases, he will henceforth bear the name of the soil god *chi no kami*. This final ceremony, devoted to the deceased as an individual, often gives rise to a special ceremony: the head of the lineage group plants the branch of a young cryptomeria tree in front of the soil god's oratory. Then, playing on the homonymy between "cryptomeria," *sugi*, and the verb "to pass," *sugu*, he declares that the time of death has passed (*sugi-mashita*). In other cases, he buries under the oratory's awning the funerary slab prepared at the Buddhist monastery to celebrate this final commemoration. In any case, the simplest way to assure that the deceased has successfully attained the status of a god is to plant a camellia branch on his tomb or next to the soil god. If this perennial plant takes root and flowers at the beginning of spring, then everyone knows that the transformation of the deceased into a god has been completed.

This affinity with death also marks the portrayals of the earth gods. Often represented by a stone, the earth god's presence is also symbolized by a five-story Buddhist tower, often seen in cemeteries, as well as in the small statue of the *bodhisattva* Jizo (Sanskrit *Ksitigharba*), which the Japanese worship as one of the intercessor spirits with the world of infernal deities. Its "divine body" is made up of fragments of a Buddhist tower randomly collected during the clearing of fields or of bones found during construction activity in the settlement: although these materials are sometimes claimed to be relics of a founding ancestor, the actual transmission of such ancient relics rarely takes place.

The spirit of the god can also reside in that large and several-hundred-year-old tree, which everyone admires and which is located near a group of several moss-covered tombs making up an old cemetery adjacent to an ancestral house which itself is located at the foot of the mountain where gods and the dead live. It is said that only the founding ancestors lie in this plot; their descendants are buried in the municipal cemetery. Some of the soil gods have demanded that a stele, engraved with the name of the violent god Kojin, be erected for them in a corner of this private cemetery. The other gods are concealed in a mound that faces in a north-easterly direction, which Chinese landscape science (geomancy) considers to be extremely dangerous because this is the direction in which the "demons' door" is located. From this border area separating the realms of man and mountain, the spirits keep watch over the destiny of their descendants. Still other gods, who are more fearful of contact with impure things, ask to be placed in the north-east corner of the residence, because it is from this direction – again according to Chinese tradition – that ancestors periodically return. They live there, at the far end of an oratory. Some have taken up residence on roadsides or, more officially, in an enclosure of the sanctuary that the village community has dedicated to *uji-gami*, the lineage god with whom these spirits are sometimes identified. However, they are also worshipped on mounds, in the middle of plots, or at the edge of rice fields, all of which are taken to be the sepulchers of founding ancestors. The living bring offerings here not only in spring and autumn, as is done for all the village gods, but sometimes also during the festival of the *bon*, which occurs at the end of the summer and celebrates the return of the dead to the village.

At one time K. Yanagita believed that the dead, who lived in the mountain, gradually began to be identified with this, so to speak, earthly beyond, and that the god of the mountain was transformed, as soon as the work season began, into the god of the fields. Finally, when autumn returned, the field god returned to the mountain, where he was once more metamorphosed into the god of the mountain. Thus the spring and autumn festivals celebrated both the return of the ancestors and the alternation of the god of the fields with the god of the mountain.[7]

The Earth God and the Agrarian Gods

This is the same earth god whom the village children, imitating the call of the fox hunters, name *kon kon,* because this ancestral god or dissatisfied deceased also has an agricultural nature: he is the messenger fox of the rice god Inari, or perhaps the god himself, or even *ta no kami,* the god of rice fields and *yama no kami,* god of the mountain, which is the winter aspect of the agricultural gods. This is why the festivals dedicated to this earth god are initially concentrated at the beginning of the agricultural season and continue until the vernal equinox. Since it is at this time of year that the sun sets directly in the west, the ancestors living in the Pure Land of the West of the Buddha Amida (Sanskrit *Amitabha*) return from the other shore (*higan* or *nirvana*) to be with the living. Identical rituals are celebrated in the autumn, season of first fruits and thanksgiving. Also at the autumnal equinox, the ancestors return once more from the other shore. Offerings of crushed rice cakes, *mochi, sake,* distilled water, or raw rice and live branches are also part of these rituals, which are celebrated in rapid fashion by the head of household alone or by his eldest son; even, on occasion, and with great solemnity, by the entire village community. In spring the children, accompanied by the village elders, collect flowering branches from the nearby hillsides. Ojichan and Obachan, Grandfather and Grandmother, grasp these branches tightly as they descend onto the plain to receive the offerings which are presented to them either near the earth god's oratory or at the altar dedicated to the dead, which is located inside the home. When fall arrives, grim-faced farmers, using sickles, chop down the *higan-bana* ("equinoxal flowers"), those enormous red flowers that grow in wild profusion at the edges of fields and in cemeteries; these absurd plants, which flower before their leaves grow and whose leaves die in the month of March, are massacred because they are believed to belong more in the other world than in this one. Rather than these flowers of the beyond, the ancestors prefer the *suzuki,* the wild grasses that wave in the autumn wind along mountain paths, resembling stalks of rice. In the Noto peninsula, following the harvest, the rice god and his wife, symbolized by two handfuls of rice stalks, are invited into the house and offered something to eat. Then they are placed next to the earth god, who is installed behind the house at the foot of the mountain, where they remain until spring.[8]

While the ancient Japanese earth gods were presented as proprietors who, willingly or by force, provided the celestial gods with the authorization to clear the land and domesticate nature, today's earth gods of the Japanese countryside not only provide the authorization to clear, cultivate, construct or destroy nature and land; they also take on the divine forms of the settlers themselves and, even more importantly, become indistinguishable from the products of the earth. Ancestors of soil and place, these gods retain the anger that they inherited from untamed nature and that makes them similar to evil spirits. Thus, as everyone knows, Kojin, especially in the form of the earth and ancestor god, has a bad temper, and his sullen mood is often the cause of a poor harvest. To win his favor, he must be periodically offered a straw rope in the shape of a snake, which symbolizes his body and represents his true nature.[9]

* * *

The personality of these gods thus expresses the imbrication of ties of blood and earth characteristic of the organization of modern Japanese society. The houses described in this paper included not only agnatic lines of descent but also all those who worked toward the preservation of the local heritage. Anyone who wanted to become a member of the village was required to establish ties of fictive kinship with one of the dominant houses and thereby become one of its branches; so much so that the terms *aiji* and *jirui* ("they who share the same land") in fact designated related persons.

The conversion of local gods into soil gods is not only, however, the result of the functional adaptation of an ancient belief to a new form of social organization. Its roots lie rather in the ancient texts, which describe how the earth gods, vanquished by the celestial deities, were forced into the other world where they were designated as ancestors. They cannot be the divinities of a prior dynasty either, because the celestial deities are the only ones who have ever held legitimate power; ultimately, their lineage merges with the divine genealogy, because they either spring from lands begotten by the celestial divinities or are worshipped for having provided wives for the celestial divinities through a system of succession based on the adoption of a son-in-law. Clearly, it is not only the ritual pact but also a shared essence between the settler and the settled that permits the settling to take place.

The belief that beings and the land on which they live are consubstantial is reinforced by the teachings of the Buddhist monks. It was they who spread throughout Japan the knowledge of the earth god Jishin, which is the Japanese form of Prthivi, lord of the gods and demons living on and under the earth, under trees, and in the vast stretches of wild and deserted land. This god, they say, revealed its submission to Buddhist law by incarnating itself in the lotus flowers that sprung up at the moment of Sakyamuni's birth. Having been converted to Buddhism, Jishin, who is also known by the name Jiten, the earth goddess who protects the law, symbolizes the fertility of the earth. As Mother Earth, Jishin promotes human longevity through its plant and also provides innumerable other benefits.

In the foundation rituals of the schools of esoteric Buddhist thought, Jishin, along with Kojin, is associated with Fudo, the Immobile One, king of wisdom. Before the earth god's sutra can be read, one must first visualize A and Om and recite its mantra. Next, the mandala of Kongokai (Sanskrit *Vajradhatu*), which corresponds to the "Diamond World," i.e. the world of outer phenomena in which the earth god lives, is drawn on the main beam of the master of the house's rooms. In this way he will assure the prosperity and security of the house as well as of the State. The ritual thus asserts that the earth god will watch over those yet to be born on this piece of soil whose strength he incarnates. In the past, when the fear of a difficult delivery was almost universal among Japanese women, it was customary for them to go, before giving birth, to the earth god's sanctuary and take a bit of soil. They then carefully placed it by their bedside in order to strengthen the spirit in their body.

As everyone knows, the fertility of the soil and the fecundity of women constitute a single phenomenon. We are not speaking here of a simple analogy between the agricultural cycle and the life cycle. The multiplicity of qualities attributed to the soil god – simultaneously wild and settler earth god, ancestor, deceased without issue and the lord of births to come – underlies the belief in the ultimate unity of the beings and things residing in a single place. To give birth or be born, to be cleared or to clear, to be dead or an ancestor: these are but diverse modes of activity in a space governed by a vital energy whose singularity strictly forbids thinking in terms of alterity. This is why the question of the ultimate nature of the earth god has no meaning: simultaneously a place, an ancestor, and a cereal, the earth god is the very substance of those who live and die there, and who are necessarily related.

Notes

1. We are referring here to *Kojiki* or *The Tale of Ancient Facts* of A.D. 712; *Nihonshoki* or *The Japanese Annals* of A.D. 720; and *Fudoki* or *The Collection of Morals and Customs*, compiled between the eighth and twelfth centuries, especially the *Fudoki Yamashiro* and *Hitachi*. Our interpretation of dogma is based on the *Shinti Daijiten* (The Great Dictionary of Shinto), 3 vols., Tokyo, 1974.
2. See on the subject, M. Abe, *Nihon no kami-sama o shiru* (To Know the Gods of Japan), Tokyo, 1989. This book is something of a catechism, describing the origins and virtues of the seventy most representative Japanese divinities.
3. Zeami, *Kadensho* (XVth Century).
4. F. Hérail, *Fonctions et fonctionnaires japonais au début du XIe siècle*, 2 vols., Paris, 1977, Vol. 2, p. 739.
5. K. Yanagita, *Minzoku-gaku jiten* (A Dictionary of Folklore), Tokyo, 1973, pp. 634-36.
6. The Fujiwara clan, which reached the zenith of its power in the tenth and eleventh centuries, offered several of their daughters to the imperial line. They also provided the Court with numerous ministers and high-ranking officials. For a time, they appeared to be the true rulers of the country.
7. K. Yanagita (note 5 above), pp. 357-60.
8. The best source of ethnographic information on this subject remains H. Naoe, *Yashiki-gami no kenkyu* (Studies of the House God), Tokyo, 1972.
9. S. Mauclaire, "The sacrifice du serpent," in: *Cahiers de Littérature Orale*, Vol. 26 (1989), pp. 83-115.

The Relationship between Society and Nature among the Hani People of China

Pascal Bouchery

With a total population of approximately one and a half million people, the Hani tribes are comprised of some twenty subgroups (the Lopi, Goxo, Zalo, Yiche, Akha, etc.), each of which possesses its own distinct identity and speaks one of the Tibeto-Burman languages. Most of this population is centered between the middle courses of the Red and Mekong rivers of China; smaller groups can be found inhabiting areas bordering on Vietnam, Burma, Laos, and Thailand. The Hani are a farming people who live in densely packed, hillside villages. Their primary crop is rice, which they grow on irrigated terraces located between eight hundred and eighteen hundred meters above sea level. The focus of this paper will be on one of the soil gods of the Hani people of the Red river area. Studying this god, who is accorded a central role in the religious liturgy of the Hani, we will see how the appropriation of a natural space and the exploitation of its resources depend directly on the cult relation maintained with him.

At the outset it should be mentioned that the Hani earth or soil gods are defined in relation to settlement; more exactly, in relation to village communities, each of which operates as a distinct religious unit. Lacking any traditional form of political organization extending beyond the village, this framework also constitutes the limit of political authority. Although it is undeniable that the various spirits associated with village life play a dominant role in the religious conceptions and activities of the Hani groups, the analysis of these spirits nevertheless runs up against a variety of difficulties. For one thing, although they are part of the celestial pantheon, these soil gods are neither contained in a defined hierarchy nor receive clear functional articulation. Moreover, their functions seem to overlap to the extent that all of them present themselves as guardians of the Hani against the incursions of evil sprits. As a result, they are presented as the source of fertility and prosperity for the totality of living beings (human, animal, and crop) living within a delimited area. In other words, these entities first appear in a protective guise, centered on a human community and its area of cultivation. Throughout this article they will therefore be referred to, in general terms, as gods – or spirits – of the "soil," since "soil" simultaneously connotes the idea of a geographic area and a of cultivated zone. Nevertheless, an analysis of the various myths reveals numerous divergences concerning the origin of each of these zones, and in the final analysis it seems that it is from this point of view that we can most easily differentiate among them.

Xama and the Hani Pantheon

The Hani, like many other Asiatic cultures, have developed a tripartite vision of the universe, establishing a fundamental distinction among three separate worlds: sky (*thapo*), earth (*thatha*), and underworld (*thawo*). Within each of these categories they establish a complex and hierarchically ordered pantheon. The authority in this spirit world lies essentially in the power of a primordial celestial divinity, conceived as transcendent, who governs – in various forms – all the spirits of all three domains. At the same time, the spirits of this world, as much in the way they are depicted as in the way they are worshipped, play an essentially secondary role and are little differentiated from each other. In fact, most religious representations of these spirits revolve around a polar opposition. On the one hand, we find a limited number of primordial celestial divinities, who are represented as omnipresent and are usually associated with the creation of the world; in this category we have the celestial emperor (Aoma, Momi) and the solar-lunar couple (Yolo/Yobö), to whom we can add divine messengers and certain lower divinities who work for and carry out orders for the supreme power. As guarantors of the universal order established at the outset of the creation, these divinities serve to protect humanity, to whose survival and development they have contributed from the beginning. Most importantly, they are thought of as spirits who are benevolent toward human beings. However, their protection is only guaranteed to the extent that humans conform, in their actions, to the norms established by these creators of the universe.[1] On the other hand, we find a variegated collection of spirits, inhabiting the earth or the beyond, whose separation from the human genus took place at a later stage of the world's creation. As a result, they are essentially of a lower order than the gods of the celestial pantheon. The relationship between human beings and these spirits, who are classed under the general term of the *tsao*, is of a more ambiguous nature and is often cast in the form of an alliance because they are above all seen as competitors who often prove to be harmful and dangerous to human beings and their goods. The Hani identify a particularly dangerous group at the center of this generic class, the *nae*, comprised of the souls of those whose deaths have been a result of demonic forces; unable to take advantage of the power of their ancestors, they become wandering souls who eternally harass the living.

Although the Hani language has no single word to designate the soil gods, as a group they occupy an intermediate position in the hierarchy linking the creator gods to the demonic forces. Indeed, from a classificatory point of view, the soil gods are in the first instance part of that variegated collection of earthly spirits, the *tsao*, among whom they undoubtedly occupy first place in the scale of values that human beings have assigned to them. However, this simple assertion covers up a key ambiguity. It is of course true that the soil gods are identified with the heavenly spirits, and in this way are similar to the primordial celestial divinities; indeed, as a tangible sign of this privileged status, their sanctuaries are constructed at the same elevation or above those of the group's settlement and fields. In this way, the soil gods are symbolically linked to the guardian spirits and ancestors. This is in contrast with the minor gods, who are identified with disorder and evil spirits and whose sanctuaries are but temporary constructions located below the settlement. However, at the same time, some of the soil gods worshipped by the Hani can, by their origin, be clearly identified with the some of the formidable and barbarous earth gods. For example, although their sanctuaries are generally located at the periphery of the inhabited area, they are nonetheless most often confined to a location outside the actual settlement. Furthermore, virtually all the Hani sanctuaries dedicated to the soil gods are made up of isolated trees or small copses, which is an additional indication that these entities originally belonged to the world of the spirits of the forest.

How, then, are we to explain the apparently paradoxical conception, which consists in the claim that the Hani worship, as equals of their ancestors, forces of the untamed world that their religious conceptions identify with the evil spirits of the forest? A succinct description of the religious representations and activities linked to the worship of Xama, the Hani soil god who plays a preeminent role in these rituals, may help us resolve this ambiguity and at the same time define the exact nature of the relations maintained by human beings in relation to this particular category of the pantheon.

Who is Xama? Although the name Xama is found throughout most of the Red River basin, the god as such is lacking in any kind of uniform religious representation. Rather, depending on which group of villages, the myths of origin associated with his name vary. Each local community worships its own god and creates a permanent place of residence for it in a tree inside a copse. This copse is always located at the edge of the village and, ideally, upstream of the first habitations. Annually, at the time of sowing, the god is made the object of a ritual of propitiation, the *Xama-tu* (literally "to offer to Xama"). The Hani attach considerable importance to the ritual and it constitutes one of the major activities of the annual religious cycle. What is at stake in the ritual is clear to everyone: if adequately propitiated, the soil god will provide a vital protection that is essential to the well-being of the community of living beings and to the resources on which the community depends. By guaranteeing the reproduction and prosperity of the living beings that inhabit the village (whether human, animal, or plant), Xama in a sense personifies the connection of a village group to its area of residence and cultivation.

Even though providing a necessary protection, Xama is not depicted by the Hani as being a benevolent figure, at least as regards his origin. Indeed, the myths associated with Xama have very little in common with those that describe the principal figures of the celestial pantheon. For example, unlike the gods of the pantheon, Xama is no way associated with the creation of the world. Rather, he is one of the *tsao*, those innumerable terrestrial spirits inhabiting a specific locale. All of the narratives explaining the origin of Xama-worship define a process akin to the pacification of a fearsome, untamed spirit, often depicted as a monstrous cannibal who destroys harvests and devours children. Originally conceived as an entity from the untamed world, whether animal or spirit, Xama appears to have been intrinsically hostile to humans; it is only by virtue of the "pact," instituted by the ancestors of the founding line of the community, that the god has in some sense been "humanized." What's more, all the myths of origin depict the nature of the original ties between human beings and the divinity to have taken the form of a contract of protection, in exchange for which the god received a sanctuary, a cult of worship, and the carrying out of periodic sacrifices in its honor.

What are the terms of this original agreement? The prosperity humans expect from Xama is in fact a direct result of the protection that he offers against all possible types of harm emanating from outside the community. Above all, the god possesses the ability to keep danger away. As he promises the Hani in a passage from the foundation myth of the cult: "If you worship me and annually offer me a pig, I will help you chase away all the other wild animals." Within the framework of this contract, the essential role of the soil or earth god is to ensure that the domain of the community, symbolized by the village fence, is not threatened by invasion from hostile forces. In recognition of this protection the community places itself in a position of dependence in relation to Xama, a fact to which the elevated position of the sanctuary – it stands above the village – bears witness. From here on, the living implore the soil god not as they would a terrestrial spirit, which is precisely what they had originally done, but as they would address their own ancestors, situated higher than they both in space and time, and from whom they expect help in return. The Hani soil god thus presents itself in the guise of a "domesticated" or "pacified" monster, but a monster nevertheless, not as some kind of benevolent divinity who participated in the creation of the world. The validity of the contract of alliance hinges on the community's veneration of the god; and because the god already exists in all places where people decide to settle, this alliance is seen as a strict obligation from the perspective of the Hani villagers.

The Soil God and the Foundation of a Village

This fundamental ambivalence in the conception of the soil god gives rise to an original way of thinking based on the idea that it is necessary, in order to make use of the resources of nature, to work continuously with the spirit world. For the Hani, in effect, the appropriation of any natural space is experienced in the first instance as a religious act by which a parcel of land is snatched from the untamed world and the spirits inhabiting it. In so doing, a living space favorable to human habitation is created; that is to say, an enclosed space which, as the Hani say, the spirits from outside "do not dare penetrate." In order to succeed at this, the Hani believe it indispensable to secure the help of the earth gods, and of Xama above all. An analysis of the rituals associated with the founding of a village reveals that the perpetuation of the alliance concluded with the divinity, along with the installation of the soil god in its wooded sanctuary, simultaneously constitute the initial condition and founding act of any human implantation on a new territory. Thus before the founding of any village can take place, a selection of the copse, inside of which Xama will take up residence, must be made. This selection of the tutelary god's sanctuary is made by divination. Another primary characteristic of the process by which the Hani found a new village is the multiplication of the divinity: the settlers must spread over the site of the new sanctuary either seeds or young sprouts from the tree which serves as Xama's residence in the settlers' village of origin.

Let us now try to describe in some detail the ways in which this ritual appropriation of a new territory is carried out. With the presumed site of the new village already determined by a process of divination (a process that implies the approval of the celestial gods), the heads of household of the emigrating families gather together in Xama's sanctuary of the mother community. After swearing loyalty to him, they then implore Xama to agree to accompany them to the new site and to protect them against the hostile forces of the spirit world on the territory in which they hope to found their new community. In return they promise to set the god up in a new sanctuary, thereby renewing the relationship maintained between them until now.

At this time, the settlers select one of their number, a man of talent, a "leader" (*axwo*), literally a "man of power," who has shown evidence of qualities acknowledged by the entire community and who, by divination, is assured to have received the support of the god. This man, selected by his fellows and approved of by Xama, plays a crucial role in what is to follow. It is through him that Xama agrees to the idea of entering into a new alliance with the group of migrants and assuring the protection of their new community against the incursions of spirits from outside it. Conferred with such authority, the leader now assumes the responsibility for supervising the series of rituals that will be required before the first houses can begin to be constructed. This job is not without serious risks, since the leader will have to rally all his powers in order to overcome the powers of the untamed world which are present on the site at the moment the migrants take possession of it.

Thus, from the outset of the foundation of a village, the act of mediation with the god is presented to us as dangerous, and demanding uncommon qualities. In fact, clairvoyance (*utse*) and force (*yoxë*) are the cardinal virtues that the *axwo* must possess. His first job is to reproduce Xama. In order to do so, he takes one of the seeds or young branches from the tree in the mother community that serves as the god's sanctuary. He then goes into the heart of a wooded area that has been chosen by divination as the site of Xama's new sanctuary and which from here on will be protected from any kind of human intrusion. Sometimes, in addition to the branch taken from the sanctuary in the village of origin, the liturgical bond linking the group of founding settlers to the mother community is embodied in a clump of earth gathered from the foot of the tree: both are placed at the site of the newly chosen mound. Once this ritual has been carried out, the settlers can consider themselves simultaneously under the protection of the gods of the sky and the earth, a condition that is required before the appropriation of the new locale can take place.

The actual founding of the village must always take place at night and preferably in winter, because there tend to be fewer spirits in winter than during the rainy season. The ritual takes the form of an armed procession, headed by the leader. To begin, the settlers go to the area chosen as the center of the new village and light a giant bonfire. This fire, just as in the myths of origin, plays an active role in evicting the spirits, because, it is said, "where ash is found, humans live." For this reason, the fire must stay lit without interruption until the first homes are built. The settlers gather around the fire, reciting propitiatory incantations. The village now possesses a ritual center (*akha*), but it is without borders. This is why this initial collective act on the site is followed by another, whose aim is to drive out, by a centrifugal movement emanating from the center, the spirits of the untamed world. This ritual eviction of the spirits, by means of which the village space is created, goes by the general name of *tsao khuu le* (spirit hunting). The participants, the number of whom must always be uneven, smear their faces with earth and turn their clothes – jackets and headdresses – inside out. They also place knives in their mouths. At the same time, the people gathered around the bonfire erupt in noise, blowing buffalo horns and banging drums and gongs. The leader, who has turned his headdress and jacket inside out like the others, now places an iron tripod – which is used for the cooking of food – on his head. This act recreates part of the myth that tells the story of the original separation of men from spirits.

Next, the members of the procession take up spears, rifles, and sticks. To these are added talismans in the form of weapons, such as the wooden knives that the Hani often place on the rope which is strung across the principal path of the village and which is reputed to have the power to keep back spirits; or those wooden forks and hammers that are the favorite weapon of Alo, the legendary hero famed for his ability to fight off demons. The leader of the group himself brandishes a bow and a broom, the latter to symbolize the act of having cleansed the site and rid it of its stench.

The leader then takes charge of the dog who is destined to be sacrificed and whose blood, along with the ash and grains of rice, will help to define exactly the border separating the inhabited site from the untamed world. Leading the procession, he begins by marching from the center first in one straight line, then in another, thereby creating two perpendicular axes; the resulting perimeter will be able to contain no less than a hundred habitations. While the procession is taking place, the *axwo*'s assistant continually spots spirits whom the head of the group pretends to kill by shooting arrows at them. In this way, the procession takes on the look of a hunt. As he walks, the *axwo* spreads grains of rice along the ground, signifying – as in the myth – that there is human habitation wherever rice covers the ground.

When a sufficient distance has been traveled, the procession stops before a large rock (if the terrain is lacking such a landmark, the participants themselves gather stones and make a pile out of them). This mound constitutes the border (*kokha*) of the inhabited world. It is here that the dog is sacrificed and its blood collected. Then the procession sets off once more, sprinkling the blood along the perimeter traced by the two perpendicular axes. Along with the dog blood, the procession also scatters handfuls of rice, ash, and metal fragments, thereby creating a boundary that will henceforth separate the human domain (*laxo-po*) from what belongs to the outside world (*lanyi-po*). Thus the village, which already had a center, now has a border as well. The Hani give the name of *misasapo* ("the place that divides the earth") to this limit. However, it is crucial that the new site not be trampled in the period just following its founding; if it is, it can become permeable again and the ritual will have to be performed anew.

Having mercilessly driven the spirits out beyond the sacred boundary, the settlers now treat them with solicitude. In effect, the human group tries to domesticate these dreaded enemies who live at the edge of their habitat. A somewhat paradoxical event now takes place: the founders of the village, who have just driven away the spirits, set about "relocating" them. A small dwelling, which resembles a human habitation and is constructed in the same manner as one, is built on top of the rock pile. At the foot of the mound the leader and his assistants offer the flesh of the sacrificed dog as well as several fowls to the gods; this in an effort to enter into a non-aggression pact with them.

The officiating priest then repeats: "Man is the elder, the spirit the younger; we were separated from each other in ancient times; the good lands are for men, the uncultivated lands for the spirits." The leader of the group places the broom, which he has carried with him, next to the dwelling of the spirits. This is to signify to them that they ought never again leave their residence. Finally, in order to compensate them for the loss of their original habitat and to soothe their potential anger, the humans suggest to the "immured" spirits that they will present them with periodic offerings of food. Thus the relationship between the human community and these spirits has gradually evolved: originally seeking their eviction, even attempting their annihilation, the human community has sought to reassure and finally to enter into a contractual alliance with the spirits. Formerly untamed, and although still possessing their demonic nature, the spirits must now yield to a new order, created by humans.

The procession then returns to the center of the village, with the leader, who is armed, walking at the back in order to keep watch for any attempt by the spirits to return. The ceremony of the eviction of the spirits ends with a ritual calling to the soul (*yula-ku*). Its purpose is to verify that none of the souls that participated in the ritual were either captured or lost. It is performed by the *axwo* in the name of all the participants.

After this ritual is completed, the *axwo* removes the iron tripod from his head, and then everyone turns their clothes and headdresses right-side out. The bonfire is stoked and will remain so until the first houses have been constructed. (If the fire were to go out, it is believed that the spirits would be tempted to try to reconquer their lost territory.) On the first night following the ritual of eviction, the settlers gather to listen for the first sound emanating from the outskirts of the village. If it is a human voice or a bird cry, it is taken as an excellent omen; however, if it is the cry of a wild animal of the forest, it means that the area has not been fully cleared of hostile spirits. The ritual of purification must then be repeated, with a new *axwo* chosen and the original location of the village center somewhat modified.

When the omen is good the founding settlers then construct the first house of the new village. This house, the front of which faces east, belongs to the leader, who has directed the entire ritual process. From the point of view of the ritual, the founding of the new site is completed with the construction of the "doors" that mark the village entrance, located at the junction of the main road and the border of the inhabited area. These doors, which serve as tangible symbols of the invisible border separating two disparate worlds, play an essential role in the termination of the foundation rituals. This is because the doors, which are believed to possess purifying powers, make possible the risk-free opening of the closed space onto the outside world. The gods that live inside or near the doors "clear" and "purify" (*sao*) both the people returning from the fields or forest and the occasional evil spirits that might be tempted to grab onto them.

In fact, the rituals associated with the founding of a village are something of a replay of the initial scene of the mythical separation of men from spirits. The bonfire, the ashes, and the grains of rice are essential elements of the original rupture as depicted in the myth, when the spirits and humans came to a mutual agreement that henceforth the lands farmed by slash-and-burn methods would become the property of the human community. What's more, the ritual performed to appropriate space recalls the trickery used by humans in the same myth, where they were able to regain the fertile lands by lighting fires all around them and by spreading rice grains over the ashes.

Viewed overall, the founding of a Hani village is an essentially religious act. A village community is formed initially not by the appropriation or economic exploitation of a piece of land, but by the creations of ties that are a result of the acknowledgment and veneration of a soil god. It is in fact the worship of a single spirit that defines a group and its land and reveals the proprietary right of the former over the latter on the basis of an ancestral contract. Such is, in this society, the rudimentary definition of property rights, the exercise of which is established above all by the celestial gods in association with the earth gods, and in particular with Xama. This framework is reminiscent of the way that P. Mus (1933) described the court of custom, which "is guaranteed by religious contract and for which property rights are secured by having access to the soil god."

In the process of founding a village, which consists above all – as we have seen – in the construction of a "rampart" to protect against attacks from outside forces, the celestial gods (Momi, Yensa) and several of the spirits of the earth (among whom are Miso and the two guardians of the "doors" of the village) play an eminently active role. But Xama, as the first soil god established on the new site, has a particularly central role in this battle. Thanks to the contractual alliance formed between Xama and the villagers at the time of the founding of the village, the potentially devastating telluric power of this ancient entity of the untamed world is, in a sense, channeled to the benefit of the village group in order to keep the hostile spirits outside the reach of the inhabited domain. The role of the leader is crucial in this action, which for the human group consists of the appropriation of a parcel of land. And since order, peace, and subsistence itself permanently depend on this occlusion of space, it is understandable that the *axwo* must perpetuate the alliance established with the soil god in order to help maintain the integrity of each of the separating limits and to assure the boundary of the microcosm. If the contract is broken, the control over the divinity is lost, and it will soon regain the destructive and savage nature it had in the beginning. This is what is at stake during the annual celebration in honor of the soil god, the *Xama-tu*, which we will now present in some detail.

The Celebration of the Soil God

The great annual celebration of *Xama-tu* is officiated by a religious figure known throughout the eastern part of the Ailao mountain range as a *migu*. Performed shortly before the annual sowing of the rice, this ritual in effect reproduces the deed of the strong man who established the original pact between the community and the soil god. The ability to renew this ancestral contract, which was entered into with a god of the untamed world, requires certain special qualities and the approval of the celestial gods. The *migu*, like the founding ancestor of whom he is sometimes a descendant, is chosen on the basis of several qualities, which the Hani first express in terms of purity (*asao*). To be the progenitor of many offspring and not to have any close relations who have had a bad death is also a sign that one benefits from the protection of the gods or, as Przyluski put it, "from a divine influence that makes him succeed." This influence, however, does not originally emanate from the divinity Xama, but from the celestial emperor (Momi) and from Yensa. Nevertheless, it is Xama who makes the final selection of the *migu*. After having narrowed the field to a small number of potential candidates, the village assembly proceeds to the sanctuary of the soil god, where the final selection is made by lottery.

The power of the village priest of the Hani is thus made manifest by the revealed action of the gods, who simultaneously incarnate the cosmic order in its totality and the village domain in its specificity. The favor of the gods of the celestial pantheon, from which the village priest benefits, provides him henceforth with an authority he can use to come to terms with the untamed energy of the earth, thereby releasing its potential fertility. The stakes here are nothing less than the reproduction of the community and its natural environment.

The etymology of the word *Xama-tu*, "to offer to Xama," refers in the first place to the sacrifice made to the tutelary divinity of the village, which is the key ritual activity of the festivities; however, the *Xama-tu* is also marked by daily oblations to ancestors, which are carried out by each household for the three to seven days that the celebration lasts. Moreover, offerings are made to the great divinities of the celestial pantheon (notably, Momi and Yensa), as well as to several earth gods other than Xama, especially the gods of the village doors. Taken together, the series of rituals constituting *Xama-tu* can be seen as an attempt at propitiating the totality of gods protecting the village space; and it takes place just before the start of the new agricultural season in order to gather together all those life forces that are linked to the village territory and to its inhabitants.

The celebration of the soil god is also linked to a complex group of ritual taboos having to do with confinement and abstinence. For one, beginning on the first day of the festivities and continuing until the last, when the village door is reconstructed, no strangers may enter the village nor any villagers leave it. During the three days when ritual activity is at its peak, the inhabitants of the community must abstain from the majority of their usual activities (field work, gardening, wood collection, etc.) and among most Hani groups women are forbidden to sew or wear hats on the day that sacrificial offerings are made to Xama. Finally, the three days of collective ceremonies are followed by a period of abstinence and rest that sometimes lasts until the day of sowing.

The celebratory activities of the second day are centered on the sacrifice, by the entire community, of a large male pig that is offered to the god at his wooded sanctuary. The night before, as a preparatory act, the village priest leads a procession of elders and musicians around the entire village, appealing to the soil god. He also carries out the annual water purification ritual, which consists of making offerings of food to the gods who are in charge of the water that flows from the spring. The sacrifice of the pig, which is carried out by the village priest and several assistants who are chosen from among the strongest and most virtuous youths of the village, is conducted in the copse in complete silence. When the group arrives at the sanctuary, the *migu* makes three low bows to the tree in which the god is housed. Then, adorning himself in a silk tunic and covering his head with a piece of fabric, the priest sacrifices the animal. Once the pig has been skinned, cut up, and cooked, some of its meat, along with other offerings of food, are put on a plate, which the priest places at the foot of the shrine. The participants then form three rows and bow to the tree while the *migu*, standing in the middle of the group, calls to Xama. With their eyes fixed on the tree, the participants then take nine steps backward, at which time they are allowed to turn away. During the sacrifice the *migu* must, among other things, inspect the pig's liver: if its small lateral appendages have a bouncy and healthy appearance, then the god has accepted the renewal of their agreement. The village heads of household, with the exception of the *migu*, divide equally among themselves the remaining meat, the head and feet being reserved for the *migu*. Some of this meat is immediately incorporated into the evening's offerings of food to the ancestors that takes place in each house; the rest will be saved until the crops are sowed, at which time the meat will be brought into contact with the seeds, since it is believed the meat has a fertilizing power.

After the offerings to the soil god have been made, a banquet is held for all the heads of household. Following this meal there is a ritual dance led by the *migu* and the community's oldest citizen. This dance, which is accompanied by the sounds of gongs and drums, symbolizes the union of male and female energies and is believed to add to the community's general fertility. The gong and drum-playing continues in a less formal manner into the evening and includes masked dances carried out by the young men of the village.

The ritual of the third day, which concludes the *Xama-tu* and the confinement of the village, consists of the reconstruction of the main door of the village. Like the day before, the *migu* is assisted by nine chosen helpers who have been culled from among the village's most "pure" and virtuous men. Early that morning these assistants visit all the homes of the village, collecting embers from each dwelling's hearth. These embers are then mixed together and used to feed the fire in which the sacrificed animals are to be cooked. The principal offering consists of a hen and two cocks that have been bought with money collected from all the inhabitants of the village. One of the cocks and the hen are presented to the gods and sacrificed together, their beaks and feet having first been sprinkled with lustral water from the sacred spring of the village. The plain-colored cock is then decapitated in the middle of the path. The cock's head is mounted on a small bamboo pole and placed just outside the village door to "terrify" the spirits.

The act of hanging the door is not a very difficult operation. This is because in regions like the Red River the Hani do not plant wooden poles in the ground but limit themselves to stringing a rope across the path, at a height of approximately two meters. The rope is made of creeping vines woven together, into which several distinct elements are inserted. In the Jianshui district there are twelve of these: three feathers from the bodies of sacrificed animals, three knives marked with black spots, three pieces of sculpted wood, and three blades of grass renowned for their sharpness. To this are sometimes added wooden hammers, which are inserted through the plaits of the rope or are hung from the horizontal cross-bars of the door when such are used.

After removing his shoes as a mark of deference to the gods "from above," the *migu* prepares a plate of offerings to be placed at the foot of the tree. Facing the sanctuary, the participants then kneel down and bow three times to the guardian gods of the door. Next, the priest removes a small portion of the ingredients from each of the ritual bowls and places these materials on the ground. Then, taking up the platter on which the bowls lie, he exits, walking backwards just as was done during the offering to Xama. Finally, at the end of the ceremony, a representative of each household removes some ash from the principal fireplace of his house and sawdust from the underside of his front door. After adding some grains of rice to them, he wraps the materials in paper and throws it away, out beyond the cord strung across the path. As he does so, he repeats the words of the original pact, concluded at the moment of their separation, which established a link between the spirits and human beings: "Everywhere where there is ash and grains of rice, there you will find men."

At the conclusion of the ceremony, the taboos linked with village confinement are no longer in force. The spring has been purified, the contract with the soil god renewed, the relations with the great celestial powers reaffirmed, the village rid of foul odors, and the protective cordon redefined: the inhabited site is in order once more. With the reactivation of the alliance with the guardians of the door, the interior space of the village can now be reopened to the free movement of human beings. Only field work remains prohibited; and this will remain the case until the *migu* himself carries out a ritual desacralization of the earth.

Having reached the end of this summary description of the annual celebration held in honor of the Hani soil god, one thing in particular has become strikingly clear: the sequence of acts making up the ritual of *Xama-tu* reproduces almost point for point the principal elements of the ritual activity that accompanies the founding of a village. As in the latter case, the officiating priest leads a ritual walk around the village. Also, as a preliminary act to the definition of the interior space, a pact of alliance, which will be repeated annually, must be reached with the soil god; this is done through a ceremony in which the soil god is installed in its sanctuary. Just as in the creation of a village, the celebration of the soil god is marked by the purification of a spring and a period of confinement which lasts until the ritual reconstruction of the village door is completed, that is to say until the limits of the enclosed space are redefined and the protection of the village perimeter assured by the reaffirmation of the links to the great celestial gods. Once the guardian gods of the door have been appropriately propitiated, the doors to the outside world can now be safely opened. Finally, in both cases the success of the alliance depends in large measure on the talent of the "strong man" who acts as mediator for the village.

* * *

To conclude, what can we learn from the special relationship that exists between the soil god and the officiant in charge of its worship? From the moment of the founding of a village site, the Hani feel the need for a man with mediative powers sufficient to establish and renew a contract with this divinity. The man they seek must be the most pure and virtuous among them, since the Hani believe that these characteristics are sure signs of the favor and grace of the gods. However, even before a man can become a candidate for this "divine mandate," he must benefit from the approval of the soil god, which is received by divination. This is why, it seems to us, that the annual celebration dedicated to the soil good is modeled on that of the founding of a village, the act which marks the original investiture of the mastered supernatural force. Indeed, it is as though the village priest, by his liturgical action, was repeating the procedure by which his illustrious predecessor had once taken possession of the village land. It is as though he were reenacting the exploit of this founding ancestor who, with the help of the celestial powers, managed to establish a pact with the soil god and to transform him into an ally of man. By his ability to harness the energies of the celestial powers – powers that influence natural phenomena and the fertility of beings – the *migu* proves to be a vector of life forces and finds himself at the center of an all-encompassing mechanism of correspondences between the village and the universe, in which he alone is the incarnation of the vital relation that determines the survival and prosperity of all.

In this way, each Hani village is an independent microcosm, centered on its *migu* and the soil god who assures the protection of the land. This unity is identically made and remade anywhere and anytime that a group of settlers sets foot on a new territory, choosing one of their own who is capable of controlling the forces of the spirit world and thereby making possible the group's access to the resources of nature. Such is the way in which the relations between the untamed and anthropized world are conceived in this society. Moreover, by the way it conceives the soil god, this society creates a coherent symbolic system in which man's action toward nature cannot be separated from his action in the religious sphere.

Notes

1. To this must be added the ancestral Manes of which the statute is a part, but which play an essential role for securing the prosperity of the living through the family cult.

The author has not systematically cited all the works upon which he has based his arguments, but they may be found in the following bibliography:

Fitzgerald, C.P., *The Tower of Five Glories*, London, 1941.
Jackson, A., *Na-khi Religion. An Analytial Appraisal of the Na-khi Ritual Texts*, The Hague, 1979.
Le, Hei, "Hanizu de Shenling Fenlei," in: *Minzu Yanjiu*, I, Gejiu, 1989, pp. 142-49. See also ibid., p. 141.
Lewis, P., *Ethnographic Notes on the Akhas of Burma*, 4 vols., New Haven, 1969.
Idem and Lewis, E., *Peoples of the Golden Triangle. Six Tribes in Thailand*, London, 1984.
Li, Qibo, "Hanizu Yuanshi Zongjiao Tanxi," in: *Honghe Minzu Yanjiu Wenji*, Kunming, 1991, pp. 11-44.
Mao, Youquan, "Yiheren Jiangshai Lisu," in: *Yunnan Shehui Kexue*, 3/1988.
Mus, P., "Cultes indiens et indigènes au Champa," in: *BEFEO*, Vol. 33, No. 1 (1933), pp. 367-410.
Rock, J.R., "The Muan-Bpo Ceremony or the Sacrifice to Heaven as Practised by the Nakhi," in: *Annali Lateranensi*, Vol. 16 (1952).

Ancestors and the Forest among the Brou of Vietnam

Gábor Vargyas

The Brou and Their Pantheon

The Brou people, whom we shall be discussing here, belong to the ancient Austro-Asiatic stock of the Indochinese peninsula. They are spread out on either side of the border separating Vietnam and Laos and settled in particular to the north of Route Nine, which joins Savannakhet (Laos) to Dong Ha (the Vietnamese provinces of Quang Binh and Quang Tri), with their area of the greatest concentration being the district of Huyen Huong Hoa (Khe Sanh) where we studied them.

One cannot discuss Yiang Su, their earth god, without first situating him within the Brou pantheon, in particular without comparing him to another important figure: Yiang Kaneaq.[1] Let us first mention that the Brou divide the gods (*yiang*) into two distinct groups: on the one hand, the *yiang tâng dông* ("the household *yiang*"), who frequent the spaces built or used by man; and, on the other hand, the *yiang tâng nsak* ("the brushwood *yiang*"), who live in the forest. While the first category has only five fixed divinities and a few other occasional ones, the number of forest deities is potentially infinite, although some recur more frequently than others in the rites. One can draw a parallel between certain entities from these two categories, and this is especially the case for Yiang Su and Yiang Kaneaq. In fact, as we shall see, Kaneaq is the equivalent among the household *yiang* to what Su represents for the forest.

The Ancestral Divinity: Yiang Kaneaq

Yiang Kaneaq is, in fact, the *yiang* of the patrilinear ancestors,[2] and more precisely of the deceased who have been absorbed into the pool of lineal divinities by virtue of their remote deaths. We should specify here that, according to the Brou way of thinking, when a person dies his "soul" (*ruviye*) leaves his body, but remains on the earth, staying close to his tomb and near the house-shaped altar (*dong nsak*) that is built in the forest for the "recent" dead.[3] In this place, after the liminal phase of a year, and on the occasion of an annual sacrifice, it joins the group of recent dead. Furthermore, each decade these agnatic dead as a whole are the object of a second funeral, which is repeated for three generations. It is only at the end of this series of very complicated funeral rites, during which the memory of the deceased becomes slowly blurred, that the soul "rises" into an ill-defined "sky," where it becomes a *yiang*, which is to say a god. The definitive rite of burial, through which this celestial ascension takes place, is called *rapup poq doq* ("burial during which the soul rises"). It is later followed by a sacrifice performed to make the soul descend from the sky, so that it might gather around the ancestral altar and fuse with Kaneaq, the divinity personifying the different generations of patrilinear ancestors.

The path followed by the "soul" of the deceased is thus circular. First it withdraws from the world of man, then eventually becomes reintegrated into it at the end of the cycle, in the form of a collective *yiang* – Kaneaq – composed of an amalgamation of anonymous ancestors from the descent group. The purpose of the funeral rites is to set this circular movement into motion, as well as to depersonalize the deceased in favor of a global ancestor. The role of this amalgamated ancestor in the creation of the unified group is fundamental, because the descent line is defined first and foremost in reference to a common Kaneaq and the group of "recent" dead who have not yet been integrated into it.

The altar of the common Kaneaq is set up in the house of the oldest member of the oldest patrilinear branch. It is at the foot of this altar that all the reunions or events concerning the fate of the group take place. Its placement in the space well reflects the superior status of Kaneaq with regard to the other domestic spirits, since his altar is placed right next to the sacred post of the house and because he is always first in a double horizontal and vertical hierarchy.

When, for marriages or other reasons, the members of the descent group leave their community, they leave behind their altar to Kaneaq, as well as the forest shelter of their not-yet-deified dead. They continue, however, to be part of the group as long as they have relatives to make offerings to the dead and ancestors of the same name. It is not until the ties with these relatives become too distant that there is a split in the descent group. This takes place during a ceremony of the second funeral. At this time, separate altars to Kaneaq and forest shelters are built in such a way as to "divide among themselves" (*tampeh*) both the deified ancestors and the deceased who have not yet become deified.

Every human being is related to Kaneaq. As a newborn, one becomes "introduced to Kaneaq" (*amut tang Kaneaq*) so that the deity recogizes him as one of his own and takes care of him. Then, during marriage, according to the rules of patrilocal residence in effect among the Brou, when the bride leaves her group to join that of her mate, she is "given away" to annul her former attachment, and then "introduced" to the Kaneaq of the group she joins. In the case of divorce, the same procedure takes place but in reverse. Finally, at the moment of death, the deceased is shifted from the care of this god to that of another, Yiang Su, about whom we shall speak later on. Everything that happens in the household or the community does so under Kaneaq's attentive gaze, be it birth, marriage, death, the construction of a new house, the arrival of a guest, or any other important event. Kaneaq must be continuously informed of everything, and if he is not he inflicts illnesses and misfortunes on members of the descent group. Consequently, there are no ceremonies during which Kaneaq is not "invited" to receive a plate of offerings; and of all the divinities he is the one most often honored, even though rites devoted specifically to him are few. Yiang Kaneaq is thus at the core of the patrilinear identity, as much as a synthetic figure of the different generations of ancestors who rules over the space inhabited or controlled by his descendants, as for his status as an omniscent and omnipotent god. At the same time he has the ability to multiply himself by virtue of the proliferation of descent groups.

The God of the Soil and of the Area: Yiang Su

Let us now examine the *yiang* of the forest, who are the main focus of this study, and in particular Yiang Su, who rules them as *yiang* of the soil and master of the entire natural space controlled by the local community. We suggested above that Su is to the natural world what the Kaneaq of each descent group is to the village. This is certainly implied in the name he is often given – Kaneaq-Su – which is also confirmed by the people themselves when they assert that "Su is the Kaneaq of the forest," or that "Su is the Kaneaq of the land [the area]."

In fact, these expressions refer to a fundamental quality shared by Kaneaq and Su: ancestrality. But whereas Kaneaq symbolizes the patrilinear ancestors, Su represents another method of organization, based on locality this time. In fact, man has more than one ancestry and thus a particular temporal origin, but he also comes from a specific place, and Yiang Su represents precisely this belonging to an area through ancestral right. Hence the simultaneous reference to both Kaneaq and the region. The central problematic of Yiang Su involves the first occupants of an area and their rights to the earth.

Here we must return to the Brou patrilinear concepts, to specify that they define themselves both in terms of descent and residence. In other words, these descent groups are localized. While in theory each village is composed of a single descent group commanding a single Kaneaq and a single forest sanctuary for the dead, in practice several descent groups usually live together. In spite of everything, each lineage is part of a larger social structure – the clan (*mu*)[4] – which has its land "of origin" where, by virtue of the rights of the first occupants, it is considered "indigenous."

The villages are spread out over the clan's territory known as the *kuruang* ("area," or "land"). Irrespective of the people belonging to other descent groups settled locally, the nominal ownership of the territory always belongs to the one belonging to the "indigenous" clan. People say that their clan "owns the land" (*yong kuteq*), and that its members are the only ones with the power to address prayers and present communal sacrificial offerings to Yiang Su.[5] In other words, its members see themselves as obligated mediators between the divinity and the people who settled in the area at a later date.

Yiang Su is conceived of as the god of the natural site since the beginning of time. He is the lord of everything that lives on the earth: mountains, rivers, animals, plants, etc. In certain ways his duties are similar to those of the "master of wild animals" as conceived of by the Siberian and North American peoples. But Yiang Su is more than this since, aside from the animals who have their own master in the person of Yiang Chih Taranh, he encompasses all of nature, both organic and inorganic. When they came to the area, humans could do nothing more than make a pact with him. On the one hand the divinity took care of them like the other creatures of the place by assuring their health, good crops, a generous hunt, and the punishment of reprehensible acts. On the other hand, they recognized his authority and guaranteed his benevolence through sacrifices and the respect of certain rules of behavior.

In short, Yiang Su is the god who, like Kaneaq in the home, "watches over" (*chao*) men, "recognizes" (*sarkoal*) them, and must be kept informed of everything that happens in the village and surrounding area. Consequently, there are no open-air ceremonies in which Su is not invited to accept sacrifices. Like Kaneaq on the domestic level, he is of all the gods of the brush the one that receives the most offerings, even though here again there are few rites organized specifically in his honor.

The members of foreign descent groups who have settled in the village clear the land and enjoy the same rights as the "indigenous" villagers, except for the right to enter into direct contact with Yiang Su. In all the important phases of the agrarian cycle, but also during all changes in the management of the space, they must invite the chief of the "indigenous" lineage (or his mandated substitute) so that he may present the sacrifice and say the prayers in their name and place. Their foreign origin is never forgotten: if they contribute to the sacrifices, they can only "nourish" (*sang*) Yiang Su, not watch over his sanctuary.

The privileged relationship between the first occupants and Yiang Su is at the core of the office of "master of the soil" played by the chiefs of indigenous lineage during certain rites linked to the working of the earth. In fact, certain phases of the agrarian cycle cannot be undertaken unless the lineal chief, who is master of the soil, has given the sign for the opening procedures. It is thus his duty to be the first to tear up an overgrown rice straw from the previous year's clearing of the land. It is also he who is called upon first to winnow the grains. In short, he introduces the spirit of the rice goddess (Abon) into the swidden plot.

Above we mentioned the sanctuary devoted to Su, but in fact the site of the worship of this divinity should be spoken of in the plural, because one must distinguish, in decreasing hierarchical order, between the clan's sanctuary, that of the founding lineage, that of the village, and finally the sanctuary of the swidden plot. These different, small shrines are usually found in a sacred grove, on the outskirts of the village, most often in a picturesque site (near a waterfall, cliffs, large rocks, for example). Another common trait is that they all contain three or four bamboo altars (*prong*) that symbolize a celestial abode, and at the foot of which rocks are placed. Two of these altars are dedicated respectively to Yiang Su and Yiang Kuruang, whom we shall discuss shortly, while the third altar is dedicated to the divinity of infectious diseases, known as "illness" (*proih*). In the village sanctuary one often finds a fourth altar, called *prong teh rana* ("the closing off [to illnesses] of the way [to the village]").

It is at village sanctuaries such as those described above that all the ceremonies conerning the territory take place. They are also the site of the two great ceremonies of the agrarian cycle involving the entire village, as well as the site of the ceremony during which Su is informed of a definitive arrival to or departure from the village. Just as one introduces the members of the descent group to Kaneaq, one "presents" all the village inhabitants to Su. The people who settle there cannot in fact clear their land until they have been "introduced" to the deity during a ceremony, which includes an animal sacrifice. In a similar fashion, as soon as someone leaves to live in another locality, he informs the Su of the village from which he departs as well as the Su of the village he joins. Dispensing with these notifications would certainly provoke Su's wrath.

As one can see, just as the altar to Kaneaq is the symbol of the descent group, the sanctuary of Su is the symbol of the local community. While the former is the site at which the unity and at times the splitting up of the descent group take place, the latter is the site at which the wholeness or the division of the local community (through the departure of some of its members) is enacted.

Divine Land Organization and the Hypostasis of Yiang Su

Let us now examine in greater detail the three types of santuaries to Yiang Su mentioned above. It is clear that the two sanctuaries on the higher level are a projection of social organization onto the spatial plane, since the first of them is devoted to the clan's territory and the second to that of the founding lineage of the local community. Since the clan is tied to a specific place through its myth of origin, the altar to Yiang Su erected on this site bears witness to the clan's territorial rights over the area. This sanctuary, called *lape kuruang* ("sanctuary of the land") or *lape put* ("great sanctuary"), is used solely for the periodic ceremonies that take place but once in a decade or when a catastrophe affects the entire population of the territory (an assassination, war, epidemic, etc.). Thus, when the Brou of the area around Khe Sanh regained their place of residence at the end of the Vietnamese war, they "cleansed" the region of all the dead who had bloodied it over the years in a *lape kuruang* ceremony. They repeated the same rite in the middle of the 1980s, but this time to cleanse the region of the contamination brought about by a fisher who lost his hand by breaking the taboo of fishing with dynamite.

The sphere of Yiang Su's influence on the level of the village sanctuaries (*lape vil*) is naturally more restricted than that of the Yiang Su who protects the clan's territory, since it includes only local concerns. These village sanctuaries are used twice a year (sometimes only once) for agrarian rites involving the local community as a whole: in the beginning of the cycle during which one "borrows Yiang Su's swidden plots," and then again after the sowing, when it is a matter of "making the rains come" (*loah doq*).

The sphere of influence of the third sanctuary, that of the clearing of the land (*lape sarai*), is smaller still: it covers merely the land cleared on the same side of a mountain. There are thus as many sanctuaries as there are groups of swidden plots. In these sites of worship, only one annual rite takes place, after the rice shoots have sprouted from the earth.

At this point in our discussion it is important to note that Yiang Su is given different names according to the levels upon which he operates and the aspects of his power being emphasized. Like the Christian trinity, Yiang Su encompasses several personalities. He is called Yiang Su when one speaks of him as the earth god in general terms. In this case he is conceived of as a spiritual power immanent to all natural elements. He is considered to dwell in the sacred grove devoted to him by his cult, but he frequents big trees as well and can appear in any place. When, on the other hand, he is conceived of as the patron of a specific territory, he is known rather as Yiang Kuruang ("*yiang* of the area") or as Achuaich Diu (Diu's grandfather). Based on these specific designations, some villagers go so far as to differentiate between Yiang Su and Yiang Kuruang, considering the former as the older brother of the latter, or seeing them as "cohabiting" (*ot parnoi*) the way the Brou and the Vietnamese do. The majority, however, think that Yiang Kuruang is Yiang Su in a different guise, that "they are identical, yet different." Yiang Kuruang is the same as Yiang Su, since like him he is within all things in nature and usually frequents big trees; but he is different from him in that he exercises his power over a circumscribed area and specifically punishes those who needlessly disturb the silence of the forest. In such cases he inflicts stomach aches or colic upon them. As yet another hypostasis of the earth god, we should mention Yiang Sarai ("*yiang* of swidden plots"), as Yiang Su is called when he manifests himself to certain men, notably to punish them for a crime they have committed.

In a certain sense these three names, as inclusive categories, can be compared to the different levels of the social structure. Referring to the divinity as it is conceived in the most general and most abstract sense as the god of the earth, the notion of Yiang Su is equivalent to the equally abstract and encompassing notion of the clan. The much more concrete level of the village community and the lineages that compose it correspond to Yiang Kuruang. And finally, with the notion of Yiang Sarai, one finds the level of the familial swidden plots and the individuals who control them.

Rich in the variety of its hypostases, the Brou divinity of the soil is likewise rich by reason of his multiple *yiang*. In fact, just as kaneaq is the amalgamated product of a multitude of anonymous dead who have become ancestors, Su gathers a mass of *yiang* associated with the two main elements of the landscape, mountains and rivers, into a single figure. "In the person of Yiang Su," said one of people we spoke to, "many *yiang* come together, and he is the chief of them all!" Indeed, these spirits are nothing more than those corresponding to the mountains and the space occupied by the local groups and the rivers that originate there.

The most remarkable elements of the Brou landscape, the mountains and rivers naturally occupy a prominent place in this population's imagination. For the Brou people, there is no mountain that is not likewise the source of a stream, and the two elements are interconnected for them. Thus when I asked about the toponomy, I was informed that terms "mountain" and "water" were synonymous. For the Brou, the mountain Ramaï and the river Ramaï are the same thing. Spatial orientation thus naturally occurs through references to mountains and rivers. The Brou use these two fundamental elements of their landscape to describe and catalogue the space they inhabit, for both practical and ritual purposes. Consequently, when someone invites Yiang Su to partake of the offerings presented to him, he includes the names of all the mountains and rivers that make up the Su of the given area in his prayer, beginning with the *yiang* of the place to which the myth of origin of the lineage's masters of the soil refers. To quote one of our informants: "First one invites the 'great Su,' (*Su toar put*), then his sons (*Su kon-kon*), then the *yiang* of all the rivers and mountains." Their enumeration also recalls the extent and limits of the region controlled by the local group.

To illustrate the procedure, let us take as an example the Bleng clan who were masters of the soil in the Coc and Dong Cho villages where I stayed. Their "great Su," which is to say their place of origin according to mythology, is a lake, the Taling Sung ("gun lake"), which is situated at the edge of the Hoong village, a few kilometers from the villages just mentioned. In the Hoong village lives the oldest lineage of the Bleng clan, and the clan sanctuary of Yiang Su is set up there. Yiang Su is thus invited to come from Taling Sung to eat the offerings; then they invite the mountains located on the territory of the family village and the rivers that originate there: Ramaï, Kul, Coc, Plang, Asing, Khel, and Saving. On the other hand the great river Nghi that crosses the Bleng territory is not invited, because it originates in the mountain Dông Pua, which is located in the administrative area of another clan.

We can gather from this example and the ideas it illustrates that spatial reference plays a large role in the identity of the local group. To this unity of people corresponds in fact a unity of worship, and thus, consequently, the Yiang Su of the Brou is a deity of both soil and area.

* * *

We began our examination of Yiang Su by suggesting that this deity was the equivalent in nature of that which Yiang Kaneaq represents for the lineages making up Brou society. We should first recall that both *yiang* personify the two modalities according to which Brou society is organized: the principle of ancestrality defined patrilinearily, on the one hand, and the idea of a locality on the other, which also refers to ancestrality, though here it is in terms of the religious preeminence of the first occupants. Furthermore, the two *yiang* are made up of many different elements, with Kaneaq including the entirety of the deified ancestors of the lineage, while Su synthesizes the *yiang* of all the local mountains and rivers. Third, Yiang Kaneaq is the supreme god of the inhabited space, the domestic sphere, while Yiang Su rules over all that is the opposite: nature and the areas situated outside the permanent control of man. But aside from their complementary relationship, the two supernatural entities present themselves as absolute masters of their realms. They know everything, watch over everything that takes place, and protect all living beings from their birth up until their death or departure. In short, the two divinities play a crucial role in the process of segmentation that results from the demographic growth of lineages (the case of Kaneaq) or of the local community (the case of Su), since they give their assent to any separation. And while Kaneaq possesses the ability to multiply himself to accommodate the proliferation of descent groups, Su possesses the same ability to accommodate the proliferation of local communities. In spite of the fact that Kaneaq embodies the principle of descent while Su embodies that of locality, in the final analysis Su also symbolizes the descent group, or clan. Only the clan is a group where, due to the ancient and presumed nature of descent, this principle gives way to that of locality.

Notes

1. *Yiang* in brou language means "spirit," "divinity," "genie." The term is similar to notions of *yang* and *yaang* that are to be found in other Austro-Asiatic societies.
2. The main unifying bond in Brou society is exogamous patrilineage (*ntang*) which is forged essentially in the course of ritual activities. The residential pattern in this society is patrilocal.
3. The more recently deceased comprise three or four rising generations.
4. The clan is distinguished from lineage in that the common origin is assumed since it cannot be demonstrated.
5. The sacrificial animals are ranked within a hierarchy that is related to their size. At the bottom one finds the chickens, then above them the pig and the goat, with the buffalo at the top of the hierarchy. The sacrifice in question here relates at least to a pig.

Portrait of the Humanist as Proteus

Michel Jeanneret

Is the perfection of a being a result of its perfectibility, that is to say its imperfection? Is the greatness of a human being a function of how much he is a man in the making? Can the human being elude all determination in order to construct itself freely or, at the very least, expose itself to an infinite number of potential destinies? This dream of absolute freedom was at times the humanists' dream. The following paper will try to show that behind the Renaissance philosophy of existence lay the principles of incompletion and transformation; that these principles were the source both of the power of Renaissance philosophy and also of its irresolution, which is what places it on the threshold of modernity.

Self-made Man

The *Oratio de hominis dignitate* by Pico della Mirandola is one of the most vigorous and influential texts of humanist thought.[1] The first part of his argument – and the only one that will concern us here – is full of optimism and is cast in the form of an encomium. Man, according to Pico, and as many others before him had already said, is an unequaled marvel in this world. What is the cause of human superiority? Instead of the usual – and, by then, worn out – theological and moral arguments marshaled over the centuries, Pico sets out to give his own answer. Reinterpreting fundamentally the creation of mankind, he is able, in a few short pages, to sketch brilliantly the foundations of a radical anthropology based on metamorphosis. Instead of reiterating the usual line of thinking, in which it is asserted that created life is lacking in stability, Pico asserts that this capacity for change is itself the principle on which human dignity rests.

In the book of *Genesis* it is said that man was created last. Pico turns to this biblical lesson and makes a completely original story out of it. According to him, the Master-Builder, his labors nearly completed, had used up his store of archetypes: there was nothing left with which to differentiate human beings from the other creatures. Adam and his descendants would thus have to make do with those attributes that had already been assigned to the other beings. God "decided that the one who could receive nothing as his own (*nihil proprium*) would have a share of all those attributes which had been given separately to each being individually."[2] Thus, according to Pico, man was to be indeterminate. Without a predefined role, appearance, or function, he would have the role, appearance, and function that he chose. He would be a being without fixed identity, but he would in return be completely free. Having at his disposal all possible qualities, he would be the architect of his own existence:

> As for the others, God said, their limited nature is held in check by laws that we have decreed: for you there is no such restriction. I have entrusted you with your own judgment, which will allow you to define your own nature ... You have been made neither heavenly nor earthly, neither mortal nor immortal; endowed, so to speak, with the arbiter's honored power of making and fashioning yourself, you can take the form that you desire.[3]

To choose one's destiny, to construct the self, to be what one wants to be (*id esse quod velit*): rarely has such a hymn to freedom been sung. The key phrases in these pages are *to want, to be able, to desire*; the dominant idea is that of a free will that acknowledges no limits. Aristotle and the Scholastics had postulated the stability of the human species, and they had attributed to man distinct and immutable attributes; although God, by his grace, could change man, human beings themselves did not have the power to escape their nature. With Pico, a voice is raised – Humanist, if there ever was one –, that disputed all forms of determinism – whether divine, natural, or social – by the power of the will.

Having not been completely created, man will therefore create himself. He "will fashion and transform himself by adapting the look of whatever animal, the qualities of whatever creature, he pleases."[4] He will choose, as he sees fit, the level of being on which he wishes to place himself: vegetal, he will be like a plant;

sensual, he will share the fate of the beasts; rational, he is suddenly a celestial being; intellective, and he becomes angelic, the true child of God. Endowed with a nature capable of these kinds of transformations, Man is a chameleon, a Proteus. And, Pico adds, it is therefore in the mythical Proteus, as in all the other stories of metamorphoses, that we must seek the essential emblems of the human being.

The fable of the human chameleon is of course consistent with a moral finality: responsible for his or her destiny, the individual must make use of this freedom for purposes of the good. But this lesson also has an ontological implication that is more important for our purposes: the greatness of a created being resides in its indeterminacy and ability to take on all possible identities. The ideal human being is a human being in the making, a malleable substance capable of fitting any mold. Paradoxically, Pico's brand of humanism is based on the absence of a specifically defined human nature. As there is no essence, no constraining model of human being, man is pure potential; having received "seeds of every kind and the germs of all types of life,"[5] it is his duty to cultivate them. There is an extraordinarily powerful image that dominates the first pages of the *Oratio*: that of a being who, exempt from all forms, is a force that nothing can stop.

The Spaniard Juan Luis Vivès is the author of another allegorical encomium of man, *Fabula de Homine*.[6] This work, probably directly influenced by Pico and certainly complementary to it, presents a somewhat less conceptually framed argument than the *Oratio* since it is presented in the form of an entertaining story.

Juno, to celebrate her birthday, invites the inhabitants of Olympus to a sumptuous meal. But the joy of the gods would not be complete without a show. A stage appears: it is the world theater, on which Jupiter will make the actors act. Among the actors there is one in particular who charms the blessed: Man. A brilliant mime, he can play all the roles: first he appears as a plant, then as various animals, finally as himself: a social creature, fair, discerning, urbane. But wait: he has not yet finished climbing the ladder of beings (this is reminiscent of that other incarnation of the Renaissance spirit, Victor Hugo's *The Satyr*, in *La Légende des siècles*). Soon escaping human contingency altogether, he takes on the characteristics of the gods themselves, before their very eyes. Finally, in his ultimate metamorphosis, he appears on stage as the splendid and powerful Jupiter himself. He is so expert at reproducing Jupiter's person that the spectators are momentarily befuddled: is this an illusion or could he in reality be the master of the universe? All that remains, in order for him to celebrate his victory, is for them to invite him to their table, to share the feast of the gods.

It is true that Vivès's conception of man is distinct from Pico's: the various existences incarnated by man are a function of a theatrical game; although he can play all the roles, he has inherited and retains the characteristic of man; he is therefore less indeterminate. Nevertheless, he has a breadth that allows him to embrace all conditions; he is like a microcosm that combines extremes, from life closest to nature to its most immaterial forms, and who gathers in one being all qualities: both the body's beauty and the infinite riches of the intellectual faculties. Pico's two analogies – that of the chameleon and of Proteus – are used here too, and to illustrate the same basic idea: man's greatness, that is to say his aptitude for spiritual life, is a function of his metamorphic nature. This is why, for better or worse, he can indefinitely transform himself; it is because he can become the equal of anything that he is virtually the equal of the gods.

In all likelihood, the Neoplatonic theory of knowledge served as the basis for Pico's and Vivès's conception of Proteus-Man. A chapter from Marsilio Ficino's *Theologia platonica* may very well have provided the philosophical foundation for their encomium.[7] Ficino's subject here is the act of knowing. All things, Ficino states, initially exist in a state of abstract form: this is the ideal model of which particular objects are the realisation. As for the human mind, he continues, it is a flexible and free organism which, "like matter, aspires to form."[8] It is thus easy for the mind to take intellectual possession of things or at least of their intelligible idea. It is by absorbing the forms of things that knowledge advances: "Only by absorbing the forms of knowable objects can the intellect have knowledge of things themselves."[9] Ficino compares this operation to alimentary consumption: just as the body, through digestion, assimilates the substance of nourishment, so the soul assimilates the model of things. Mental absorption is in fact easier than material absorption; while material substances present physical resistance to the act of union, ideal forms pass unhindered into the intellect. Consequently, knowledge is based on fusion: "From our intelligence and from the form of the intelligible object there results the individuated thing."[10]

It follows from this theory that the soul is capable of assuming the form of anything. More than that, its very purpose is to become anything: "The intellect more or less becomes the thing it understands. It becomes, I say, this thing in act ... ; this actualization is the very act of understanding."[11] Infinitely receptive, the soul can therefore experience all categories of knowledge and all modes of being. To illustrate this metamorphic nature, Ficino enumerates, and classes in ascending order, – just as Pico and Vivès will do later – the different lives the soul is capable of living; from the vegetable kingdom to the divine, from the state of an animal to that of a human, from the heroic to the demonic and angelic. Moreover, this analysis of the soul can be applied to man himself, which makes it possible to move from epistemology to anthropology: "The human genus strives to become all, because it leads every type of existence."[12] Although Ficino's aim is clearly metaphysical – to inspire in created beings the will to become God –, it also implies a general conception of existence that, in order to assure the greatest possible mobility for the intellect, offers man every possible kind of transformation.

"We Are Never in Ourselves"[13]

Both Ficino with his fusional conception of knowledge, and Pico and Vivès with their fervent vision of Man ascending the steps of the ladder of beings, constructed theoretical fictions. Yet the distance separating their speculations from the lived experience of certain humanists is not all that great. In fact, there were numerous Renaissance figures who, as if sharing the philosophers' ideal of an existence capable of multiple mutations, adopted the principles of variety, mobility, and change as a basis for living. In order to demonstrate how the spirit of metamorphosis inspired the behavior of many and had a bearing on the fate of more than one

Renaissance figure, I propose to sketch (with an emphasis on my announced theme) the portraits of two pivotal figures of Humanism – one of its early figures, Petrarch, and one of its leading representatives at its acme, Erasmus.

Petrarch, during the entire Renaissance, was viewed as a founding father and a model to be imitated. What style of life did he in fact bequeath to the humanists?

A fervent scholar, he liked nothing more than to devote himself to his beloved studies: reading and writing, philological labors and meditation, all of them carried out in calm and protected surroundings. And yet he never succeeded in locking himself up in his ivory tower for long periods of time.[14] Instead, he ventured forth abroad, took part in public life, and engaged in a variety of activities, all the while criticizing his own versatility and always yearning for his studious retreat. The tension between *otium* and *negotium*, between the contemplative and active life, determined both his self-consciousness and the rhythm of his activity. Striving for stability, Petrarch, in spite of his will, found instability; desiring unity, he succumbed to multiplicity. Whether intentionally or not, this inspirer of European humanism already manifests the metamorphic tendencies of the chameleon.

As a scholar and writer, he was curious about everything, offering to the observer the profile of a man of letters with a remarkably diverse and changing range of interests: a philologist and editor devoted to the Ancients, but also a historian, moralist, letter writer, without even taking into account his poetic activity, which itself encompassed epic, bucolic, and lyric forms. Although he wrote primarily in Latin, his love poems were composed in Italian, and he experimented in a wide variety of genres and styles. Thus, without even rising from his writing table, he had already demonstrated a remarkable multifacetedness. But how could he cut himself off from the world when there were manuscripts to be searched for, collected, and studied the world over? And what about the necessity of arranging for the publication and distribution of one's own works, not to speak of the pursuit and, ultimately, the attainment of the official stamp of poet laureate?

What is more, Petrarch was not captive of his books: interested in contemporary events, he took public positions, which added to his range and breadth. His immense correspondence, to be remembered as one of his greatest literary works, shows him to be surrounded by a vast network of friends and preoccupied with a thousand moral, literary, and political questions. As efficient as he was in managing his literary affairs, he also gave himself over to the public arena; charged with diplomatic missions, he was a friend of the powerful – emperors, popes, and local leaders – and on occasion played a role in the affairs of the state of the fourteenth century. And how could one forget the *Canzionere*, in which a totally different side of Petrarch becomes visible; that of the lover obsessed by his passion, his love for Laura, which becomes an expression of his love for the Supreme Good?

This kind of polymorphic activity finds its most clear expression in travel. In his mature years Petrarch never remained in one place for long. Explorer or exile, pilgrim of God, science, or politics, Petrarch was drawn on by his curiosity. He zigzagged around Italy and Provence, but also traveled to northern Europe: Paris, Cologne, Basle, Prague ... . There is an enormous contrast between this vagabond mood and the traditional tranquillity of the sage or monk, with which Petrarch nevertheless felt kinship. Indeed everything seemed to predispose him to a contemplative and sedentary life. However, something inside him apparently gave way, turning him into a multiple being, a wandering and manifold man in whom posterity perceived a restless being, a man torn from himself by the flux of events; or, to put it in less negative terms, an exemplar of that openness and flexibility of spirit that are so many signs of freedom. Petrarch's psychological and intellectual mobility is perhaps an indication of early modernity; in any case, it surely heralds the advent of a conception of life that enjoyed great popularity during the Renaissance.

In Petrarch's philosophy of existence we can thus see in outline something resembling "existential phenomenology."[15] Those humanists prefigured by Petrarch are, either literally or figuratively, travelers, seekers and investigators; their concern is less with constructing a coherent identity or oeuvre than it is with taking their quest of adventure to its limit – a quest for the other and a quest for one's self. Their acts of introspection and self-portraiture do not depict – or only with great difficulty – a unified and consistent entity: although the inner self is ardently desired and sought, it appears to be vulnerable to disintegration by aggressive energies, to fragmentation by centrifugal forces. The human person, as conceived by many humanists, is but a sum of heterogeneous elements (events, moods, social pressures), the terms of whose unstable equilibrium must be constantly redefined. It follows from this that the self, far from constituting a distinct and homogenous subject, occupies a zone of openness and mutability, in osmosis with the outside world. Man, adaptable and permeable, exposed to contingency, is conceived as a constantly mutating system. Whether this dispersion of the self is experienced as a form of loss or sorrow, or as the normal result of a joyously expanding force, the basic perception of a changing, disjointed, and aleatory existence remains constant.

Erasmus's itinerant destiny is well documented. Constrained by circumstance, curiosity, and need, attracted to and then repulsed by dependency, he never stopped moving; so much so that his friends, who were dispersed over all of Europe, complained of losing track of him. His friend Ambrogio Leoni wrote to him from Venice:

> I heard it said that you died in France; a few years later, that you had come back to life in Germany. Later, that you were being mourned in Germany; and still later that you had been seen arriving in Italy. Finally, I learned on good authority that you were dead in England and just had struck out for France from Avernus.[16]

Disappearing in one place only to resurface somewhere else; dying here only to be reborn there; this series of migrations, Leoni writes, "gives me the impression of observing a new Pythagoras." He continues, quite naturally invoking Proteus:

> Not only from an Italian, you were observed turning into a Frenchman; from a Frenchman you became German, as if a bird had been seen arising from a calf, and from a bird some kind of corn ... . But from a poet you changed into a theologian, and from there metamorphosed into a philosopher of the Cynical school; and the final change: you traded in the Cynical philosopher for the role of an orator. Only Proteus could be the author of such a multitude of shocking transformations. And indeed, as I look now upon the books you've had published, I can see how you have varied the known forms and appearances of your person and talent.

Erasmus's correspondent then adds that the readers of his books have taken all his "metamorphoses" to mean that "they are the work of three or four authors."

Erasmus's answer betrays a certain indecision. He begins by rejecting the notion of "natural inconstancy" as applied to him: "Amidst all the upheavals Erasmus remained the same and absolutely identical to himself."[17] Yet at the same time he acknowledges the unhappy fact of his nomadic life, doomed to turmoil and the unexpected: "My evil genie put me to a test that had more perils, more wanderings than Neptune imposed upon Homer's Ulysses." Although accepting the comparison with Pythagoras and Proteus, he nevertheless takes it as a reproach and blames it on the theater of social life: "As soon as I began to play one role I had to take another." Beneath the masks and accidental roles the wise man claims to remain one. However, from the public's point of view, he is Proteus.

As Leoni expresses it, the impression of mutability produced by Erasmus is as much a result of his writings as it is of his constant travels. Just when it seems that Erasmus has been pigeon-holed in one specialty, he is already somewhere else, prospecting some new strip of land. Erasmus confides to a friend: "If a man wishes to make a name for himself as a writer, the key is to choose a subject suited for his natural gifts and talents, because not all subjects are right for everyone. And that's what I could never do."[18]

Erasmus made this confession in 1523 as he was preparing, for the first time, an edition of his collected works. To organize such a diverse body of work he catalogued, in this same letter, everything he had written to date and divided it into nine categories. These nine categories were to comprise the nine volumes he envisaged: 1. Didactic Manuals for the Teaching of Letters, 2. *Adages*, 3. Epistles, 4. Moral Treatises, 5. Pious Works, 6. Translation of the New Testament and Notes to it, 7. Paraphrases of the New Testament, 8. Apologies and Polemical Discourses, 9. Edition of the Letters of Jerome.[19]

Erasmus lived an additional thirteen years after drawing up this list: plenty of time to augment the variety and versatility of his intellectual biography. Never satisfied, always carried forward by curiosity, he constantly supplemented, deepened, and explored new avenues. A tireless laborer, compulsive and hurried, he felt himself involved in a vast enterprise, comparable, as he wrote, to the labors of Hercules.[20] The centrifugal tendency in Erasmus is especially perceptible because of the fact that throughout his entire career he worked in two immense and almost irreconcilable fields; simultaneously a disciple of the Ancients and a witness to the truth of the Gospels, "the Christian of *the Enchiridion*, the pagan of the *Adages* and the sage of the *Colloquia*."[21]

Erasmus never made a final choice between service to the Word and his love of ancient literature, even though, depending on the period of his activity, the emphases vary. Why should Greco-Roman civilization be ignored, when its models of wisdom and style did so much to improve human life and develop man's power? At the same time and even more so with its passage, how could one not devote oneself to the understanding and dissemination of the Holy Scriptures, and to the restoration, inside the Church, of the spirit of Christ, without which our actions remain vain and sterile? He wore the hat both of the theologian and the man of letters, not to mention all the other ones. Luther said of Erasmus that he was slippery as an eel.

A Proteus of the pen, he was also one in character. He detested commitments and avoided ties of all kinds, whether it meant acceding to the will of another person or giving undivided loyalty to an overly constraining cause. Herein lies one of the causes of his constant peregrinations: in order to avoid a lasting obligation to any single protector, he passed from one to another. What about the increasing number of disputes among schools of thought, nations, and faiths? And the growth of fanaticism of all kinds? Erasmus found a way around them. In the field of the humanities, for example, he manifested complete independence: while advocating the study of Antiquity, he criticized the paganism of certain scholars and aesthetes; he fought for the return to classical Latin but rejected Ciceronian purism. However, it was in the religious sphere that he showed the greatest versatility. Although mercilessly criticizing and fighting to change the Roman Church, he nevertheless remained faithful to it; opening the way to Reform and actually fellow-traveling with the Protestants in part, he nevertheless refused to become a member of any new Church. Navigating between extremes, he was an excellent conciliator and thereby earned the censure both of the Catholic hierarchy and Luther: both sides called him lukewarm, pusillanimous, a traitor.

This labile man was drunk with freedom: opposing Luther, he was a ferocious defender of free will, seeing it as the foundation of moral life.[22] He would probably not have repudiated Pico della Mirandola's image of man: he, too, is a Proteus, capable of all kinds of metamorphoses and open to all experience; acknowledging his intellectual mobility, he demands the right to spiritual disquiet. Flexibility, for him, is not necessarily a weakness; it allows him both to incorporate every possible means of improving life here below and of climbing the ladder that leads beyond, to God.

Educate, Form, Cultivate

Erasmus ascribes this capacity for change to all human beings: "*Homines non nascuntur, sed finguntur:*"[23] humans are not born completely formed, their being is not predetermined by innate characteristics, but rather they come into existence as a substance to be shaped. Once again the Dutchman's view coincides with Pico's: we are dealing here not with essence but rather with existence that must be constructed, potential to be realized. Erasmus's interest in pedagogy is a natural outgrowth of this dynamic conception of the human individual. If the human being is malleable, then it is crucial for the philosopher to orient him or her toward the good: service to society and the love of God. It is precisely this concept of human malleability – the receptive and pliant infant is viewed as born to be molded – that explains the presence of a didactic strand in Erasmus's works: manuals for learning Latin, a treatise on good manners, and a plethora of moral precepts.[24]

This principle governs much of sixteenth-century thinking. There was hardly a single area of human activity, it was believed, that could not be formed, transformed, and reformed by the appropriate intervention. This program is implicit in the very idea of the Renaissance: if culture is to be restored and life improved, men must be prepared to face new challenges; they must themselves be changed in order to change others; they must adapt themselves to abandoned Biblical and Ancient models so that they in turn could inculcate these values in future generations. Already at the beginning of the fifteenth century, the humanist Vergerius was exhorting parents to begin the education of their children at the earliest age possible in order to take advantage of the natural flexibility of youth, "while their mood is malleable and their age pliant."[25] *Mobilis aetas*: whether speaking of the age of an individual human being or, by analogy, of an entire human society, this formula well expresses a basic tenet of the humanists: in life as in history, moments arise that are particularly propitious for shaping – like so much ductile matter – the individual or the collective. It is at such moments that intervention is required.

It is significant that the word "culture," in the sense of "the development of intellectual capacities," initially arose during this period. Up until then it had been largely restricted to the vocabulary of agriculture, and it was only applied metaphorically to matters of the mind. Du Bellay praised the Greeks and Romans for having been "diligent in the culture of their Languages,"[26] while Montaigne spoke of "the culture of the soul."[27] Later all reference to labors of the land disappeared and the modern meaning of the word took firm hold: "he is a man of great culture," "French culture," etc. During the Renaissance, this figurative dimension of "culture" ensured its dynamic import: "culture" was not a given, it was acquired, and as acquired it required work, action upon the spirit, a transformation of the given.

Because the mental faculties had to be shaped, it was only natural that the number of instructional treatises increased. Although some of these treatises took up education in general, many specialized in particular skills. Young men were trained for public life: how to become a prince or courtier, how to speak and comport oneself correctly in society.[28] The path to spiritual perfection and the practices of religious rigor were described.[29] Professions and technical skills were also taught: how to use arms, the secrets of the hunt, dance steps .... The sheer volume of this pedagogical production, accelerated by advances in printing, is indicative of humanist optimism: it is as though there are literally no limits to the absorption of new capacities.

But are there limits to what can be learned? Is the individual truly a blank slate, an infinitely malleable ball of wax on which any form can be impressed? Or are there innate propensities and inner resistances that tend to reduce the scope of potential or even desirable achievements? Are we thus speaking of formation from nothing or rather of transformation of something? The opposition between Rabelais and Montaigne on this point shows that when it is a question of the scale of the student's transformation, there is more than one doctrine. A comparison of their pedagogical programs reveals that there are in fact two anthropological outlooks within the same will to fashion man.

After having vegetated under the harsh rule of the old school – that of the "old coughers"[30] of the Age of Scholasticism –, Gargantua is finally exposed to humanist knowledge, under the enlightened tutelage of Ponocrates. From dawn until dusk, "he doesn't waste a single moment but spends all his time in studying letters and the sciences."[31] There is so much to learn, such a constant stream of lessons and exercises, that he is unable to keep up with his own oversaturated schedule. Everything must be known: not only Man, the world, and God, but the arts, sports, and practical things. The aim is to be able to do everything. Ponocrates's program encompasses all spheres: body and soul, intellectual and manual labor, religious and profane life, the social and natural sciences, theory and practice, work and leisure ... Gargantua's madcap day takes on the look of a catalogue *de omni re scibili, et quibusdam aliis*. Under the pretext of offering an education Rabelais seems to be setting forth the outline of an encyclopedia: surveying everything to be taught, he assigns his student a limitless field of inquiry, as if he were giving his hyperbolic and fictive version of the ideal of openness and totality that Petrarch and Erasmus incarnated in reality.

Chapters twenty-three and twenty-four of *Gargantua* fulfill this function to the extent that we read them as Rabelais's attempt to summarize his ideal of a total pedagogical program. If, however, they are read as a practical guide and model, then they can only be judged an aberration. It is clear that Rabelais is little concerned with verisimilitude and even less with psychological coherency. There is no attempt to adjust, and no perceptible correspondence between, the active subject of the apprenticeship and the objects of instruction. Rather, the student absorbs all, immediately and without differentiation. He has no effect on the material and there is nothing to suggest that he either internalizes or is changed by it.

Quantity wins out over quality, and memory, which swallows up all the data without distinction, leaves no room for a critical attitude. Gargantua offers himself to Ponocrates as a blank slate on which any message, that is to say all possible messages, can be imprinted. The education to which he acquiesces can therefore include everything; and because he has no individual character, he can offer no resistance to this pedagogical saturation. Infinitely passive and receptive, he resembles that indeterminate being, that candidate for every imaginable metamorphosis, which Pico della Mirandola had defined as the essence of the human.

Taking charge of his student, Ponocrates immediately turns to a doctor

> who canonically purged him with Elebore of Anticyre, a medicine that washed away all the alteration and perverse habits of the brain. By this means Ponocrates caused him to forget everthing he had learned from his former teachers.[32]

Erase and begin anew. Stripped of his preconceptions, freed of his bad habits, Gargantua can be reborn, as virgin and pure as a Phoenix. No form of the past – neither previous experience nor psychological inheritance – can have any effect on the new state of affairs. The purgative causes a radical rupture in the life of the giant: Gargantua before and after are two distinct beings.

There are two, or perhaps several, Gargantuas. One need only to look at the description of the early stages of his life and education to note the discontinuity of character and the rupture of the psychological subject – or rather its absence. Instead of a cumulative and progressive path, moments simply follow one after another, as if at each stage the narrator was describing someone different. The group of chapters devoted to the giant's youth can be divided into three phases: infancy, which is marked by the spontaneous flowering of his body and mind (chapters 7 and 11-13); a vegetative phase, under the influence of the Sophists of the Gothic period (chapters 14 and 21-22); and finally, under the tutelage of Ponocrates, a period marked by stunning progress (chapters 23-24). Is this the same young man who had been developing gradually? The impression is rather of three independent episodes or three juxtaposed systems, which does not accord well with the ideal of a single, unified, evolving individual.

In addition to this kind of discontinuity, there is another, which is observable in the first two phases. Already in infancy we can note two tendencies that are difficult to reconcile: while Gargantua abandons himself fully to his sensual appetites, busy only with eating, drinking and sleeping, he nevertheless gives evidence of ingenuity both in the game of wooden horses and in the invention of ass wipes. Yet hardly has he shown a flicker of intelligence than he falls immediately into the most abject stupidity: regressing, he begins again to stagnate, even wallowing in the mud, which somehow does not prevent him from engaging in farces that make everyone forget his foolishness (chapters 16-20). Thus, simultaneously and on two separate occasions, it is as though distinct persons coexist within the same body, producing a portrait whose psychological unity is no more convincing than the chronological one described earlier.

This fragmentation of character can be found elsewhere in Rabelais. What does the Panurge of *Pantagruel*, adventurer and wag, have in common with the one found in the *Tiers* and *Quart Livres*, sophist and poltroon? How are we to reconcile the Pantagruel of the novel's end – wise and meditative – with the young giant of the beginning? Although there are some constants, it is the dissonances, differences, and even contradictions that are most striking. These fractures in the construction of individuals – even if fictive individuals – imply a particular conception of man. Character is not conceived of in terms of a uniform and consistent subject, and life does not necessarily follow a linear evolution. Instead it is presented as a series of separate and rather loosely linked moments, a montage of poorly integrated episodes and actions that fails to constitute a coherent personality. Man is discontinuous because his life is composed of a sum of events that are themselves discontinuous.[33] Not having to suffer the weight of the past nor anticipating the future, he is completely encompassed by the present moment, totally identified with the role he is currently playing. During one period of his life Gargantua is completely the student of the old coughers, a pure product of Scholasticism; only a little while later he will be Ponocrates' obedient disciple, a consummate incarnation of the humanist spirit. Just like Pico's created being, he is a chameleon; merging with the surrounding landscape, he is what circumstance makes of him.

The history of narrative forms would seem to confirm this fragmentary and metamorphic vision of existence. The French sixteenth century has left us few long novels: the potential of the great Chivalric collections of the Middle Ages went largely unexplored during this period while the long heroic narratives of the seventeenth century had yet to appear.[34] There is a probable correlation between fictional characters of short duration and the absence of long, complex narratives. This seems especially convincing in light of the fact that the short story (French *nouvelle*) was the most fashionable genre of this period – the *Heptaméron* of Marguerite de Navarre and collections of brief narratives were widespread. Significantly, the short story rarely tells the story of an entire life. Rather it seizes a crucial moment – an adventure, a news item, a moment of passion – in the life of a character. Instead of detailing a complex chain of events or the evolution of a character's psychology, the short story captures a character in a moment of defining action, in the midst of a singular and self-contained situation. Generally speaking, Rabelais's novels have a *modular* structure, which is particularly visible in the *Tiers* and *Quart Livres*. This form, which operates by juxtaposing similar episodes without any relation of cause and effect, can be compared to the compositional structure of the short story.

Montaigne too had a lot to say about the question of formation and transformation. Although he agreed with many of the premises of his contemporaries in regard to the receptivity of the student and on the mutability of man in general, he tended to diverge from them when it came to the principle of indeterminacy and tried to limit the scope of the metamorphic principle. He approached the infinite mutability of Proteus with suspicion. The chapter devoted to "the institution of children" bears witness to this reserve.

Let us begin with the points of agreement. According to Montaigne, the young child is a malleable substance whom the teacher endeavors to shape: molding his student's powers of judgment, will and morals, the teachers imparts to him the qualities of a gentleman. By methodical and determined action the student undergoes a decisive change. Montaigne envisages applying various strategies, which can result in a double transformation: "Borrowing things from others, he [the student] will blend, alter, and transform them, making them his own, that is, his own judgment. The sole aim of his school, work, and study will be to form this faculty."[35]

To sharpen his critical skills, the child will be encouraged to appropriate and make use of the classics as he sees fit: the subject himself is modified in the process of modifying the object of study. Elsewhere in the same chapter the combination of changes is described as conforming to yet another mechanism:

> I often admiringly noted Alcibiades' marvelous nature, his ability to transform himself so easily and in so many different ways, without any concern for his health: first surpassing the pomp and sumptuousness of the most elegant Persian; then as austere and frugal as any Lacedomonian; as effortlessly a reformed Spartan as a voluptuous Ionian ... . This is exactly how I would like to mold my disciple.[36]

Instructing the child in the chameleon's stratagem, teaching him to transform himself: it is education that gives the impetus to the first of many metamorphoses of the self.

Montaigne thus largely acknowledges that the very principle of education is based on the pliability of the human spirit. In this context, it would be naive to be surprised by his speaking of mobility. What is surprising, however, is to see him equally insisting on the necessity of stability. The teacher, he says, does not operate on a blank slate. Rather he addresses a subject who, although malleable and receptive, nonetheless possesses a unique character, distinctive qualities, and an already established personality. Montaigne speaks freely of the "nature" of his student, of his "form," his "inclinations," and his "natural proclivities." He insists on the existence of a solid and inalienable center at the very heart of the individual; and if this center can not be said to be literally resistant to change, it does furnish limits. Without such a barrier the self rushes headlong and rudderless, losing its bearings and ultimately evaporating.

Montaigne, unlike Rabelais, does not think of education as operating on virgin soil. Rather, it either reinforces or counteracts already existing tendencies, actualizes preexisting capacities, develops a potential. Are these characteristics innate or acquired? Are they immutable or subject to change? The fact that Montaigne's answer to this question is unclear is not crucial. Whether our "form" is fixed once and for all by God or Nature, or whether it develops over the course of life, it nevertheless exists; and even if this form is but rudimentary and vulnerable to all life's contingencies, it nevertheless precludes the radical instability of Proteus. It is significant that in this chapter on education Montaigne avoids the themes of inconstancy and discontinuity that are generally so present in the *Essays*.

Where does the fluctuating part of man end and the constant part begin? Montaigne's hesitancy to answer this question definitively constitutes an essential element of his thought and is manifested, among other ways, in an ambivalent (one might even say muddled) attitude toward the very idea of "form." Montaigne is suspicious of the scholastic concept of form. As he writes: "Others form man; I describe him, and myself present a particularly badly formed example of him."[37] This formative activity, which he leaves to the philosophers, postulates the existence of an essence, a universal model – Aristotelian form – to which all individuals must conform. Yet, Montaigne argues, this concept of an invariable mold, transcending the accidents of history, is a mere abstraction, an invention of metaphysicians whose theories are removed from reality. This form, fixed and artificial, stereotyped and normative, denies the dynamism of freedom and constitutes an act of violence upon the individual which Montaigne rejects. Yet this does not prevent him from writing elsewhere: "I put all my efforts into building [French: *former*] my life. This has been my profession and my labor."[38] While the "others" have imposed an authoritarian model of man, a congealed and predefined standard, the I gropes around the central kernel, that is to say, empirically, within itself, which it needs to do in order to act and know itself. The apparent contradiction in the two statements above can perhaps be resolved by observing the first person conjugation of "building life" (*former la vie*), which here means to seek and construct oneself; it is thus a legitimate act, a quest for a future object, and perhaps an infinite process. Nonetheless, the ultimate aim is to find and establish a form that will enable the subject to coincide with himself. As a result, with a clear conception of his or her "nature," he can simultaneously increase his self-knowledge and his power to lay down a coherent course of conduct.

This theme, along with the two-sided concept of "form," underpins another chapter of the *Essays*, "On Repentance."

Reduced to bare bones, the argument is simple. The text opens with the above-quoted statement from the "badly formed" one, then offers a most beautiful and radical image of the concept of universal and personal flux: "The world is but an endless seesaw ..." [39] Will this self, exposed to the discontinuity of time, be engulfed by moral anarchy? Montaigne says no. And this is because there exists an inner consistency inside of man, a kind of model on which he can base his actions; this norm allows him to settle on a code of behavior and to avoid repentance. Having recourse to his "governing form,"[40] he can develop an authentically personal ethics, free of the factitious prescriptions of the moralists. The content of this inner substance remains undefined. It is designated in various ways – "the inner guide," "natural inclinations," "native condition," "original characteristics," "one's own form," "universal form"[41] – and perhaps implies nothing more than an acknowledgment of the mobility of human being: although I have no stable form, my instability itself is the form with which I coincide.

Thus begins to emerge an image of the self that obviously includes malleability and fragmentation but which is identical neither with Pico's Proteus nor Rabelais's blank slate. While sharing in the *perpetuum mobile* of the Renaissance, Montaigne seeks in himself and attributes to the other a kernel that is untouched by indeterminacy. Experiencing his variability as a shortcoming of being and a sign of vanity, he connects the precariousness of the human condition to an ontological insufficiency. His position constitutes a crucial stage in the history of the conception of the subject. With Montaigne, and more and more after him, the concept of human dignity becomes bound with the notion of inner consistency, of a being resolute in its resistance to change. The Renaissance had seen mobility, the capacity for an infinite variety of metamorphoses, as man's special privilege. Henceforth the human person would be perceived as a solid and independent entity, with a unitary center and a fixed point of reference. This demand for continuity and coherence would prevail for many centuries, concealing or rejecting the metamorphic sensibility of the sixteenth century.

The Joys and Sorrows of Metamorphosis

In celebrating change as a sign of human greatness, Pico and Vivès, unlike Montaigne, took metamorphosis to be a blessing; it symbolized the powers of human being, its freedom and openness. The moral interpretation of Proteus, evident in the mythographies of the Renaissance, gives a clear indication of this.[42] In his *Mythologiae sive Explicationes Fabularum* (1551), the Italian scholar Natale Conti attributes, as had other commentators, both Ancient and Renaissance, several possible meanings to the sea god. A few quotes should suffice to demonstrate the range of merits he associated with metamorphosis. To begin with, Proteus is celebrated as the very incarnation of the man of learning, well versed in matters of natural sciences, who "wrote a host of treatises on philosophy, botany, and geology; on the nature of the animals and the mutual mutation of the elements; and on how from these all creatures draw their beginning and, growing, become trees or herbs or animals."[43]

To progress, like Proteus, from one existence to another is tantamount to having inner knowledge of the life of the various species and a better understanding of their natural mutations. The truly learned man is one who can mentally enter into the heart of things and participate in their mobility; his instability is proof of his veracity.

As for himself, Conti continues, he would rather see in Proteus the mark of a good leader; one who can, in civil administration, maintain harmony among men. Society is composed of men of various temperaments and of conflicting forces; it therefore requires a leader who, in order to mediate among them, knows how to listen:

> It is therefore necessary that the Wiseman be one who does not so much take pleasure in any particular activity – because in society not every man takes up the same occupation – but who can, by various disguises, enter into cordial relations with all men and by a diversity of means manage the multifarious interests of the State.[44]

Because of his ability to adapt both to men and events, Proteus-the-Sovereign is simultaneously a mediator and a moderator. Able to be everything to everyone, he symbolizes tolerance, mutual understanding, and peace. Yet, Conti adds in conclusion, the applicability of this fable is not limited to the political realm: it can serve as a general model of "human life." Proteus teaches us to balance opposites, to avoid excess and to arrange our activities in accordance with the golden mean. Having himself passed through every form of existence, he knows that there is room in us for every possible kind of experience, tempered by the *aurea mediocritas*. Vincenzo Cartari, he too a mythographer, summed up the lesson of Proteus in a single phrase: "His great wisdom consisted in his ability to adjust to all things."[45] By having developed man's metamorphic power to its maximum, Proteus found himself promoted to the rank of master of life, protector of society, and guarantor of civilization.

Human self-realization therefore depends on self-multiplication and on the assumption of as many incarnations as possible. Ronsard too makes use of the metamorphic myth in order to express this ideal of totality. He addresses the following sonnet to his teacher, Dorat:

> Aurat, after your death, the earth does not deserve
> To rot such a learned body as yours truly is.
> The Gods will change it into some voice, or else
> If Echo isn't good enough, they will change it into a swan,
> Or the horn that lives on dew divine
> Or the bee that makes Hymatian honey,
> Or the bird that sings the ancient crime
> In spring, of Teree, retold on a thorn
> Or if you've not been completely changed into someone
> You'll be dressed in a horn shared
> With the others, participating together
> And all (because one is not enough for you)
> From a man you'll be made a beautiful new monster
> Made of voice, swan, cicada, of fly and of bird.[46]

As a kind of recompense, the learned man will experience the joys of alterity. The beginning of the poem, with its disjunctive enumeration of potential transformations – either this or that – gives way to an additive order – both this and that – signaling that full self-realization is reached only when the subject, instead of choosing, is himself multiplied in simultaneity, both one and many, self and other. The airy lightness of the self's avatars – voice, insect, bird – reinforces even more strongly the impression of mobility and freedom. Unlike Ovid's depiction of metamorphosis, which is usually associated with violence, suffering, and passion, Ronsard depicts the migration of the body as a triumph of life. He also confers a positive value on the "beautiful monster," a traditionally negative symbol: what was once a deformity bearing the imprint of error, or a threat to order and a troubling omen, now becomes the perfection of a polymorphic existence.

The metamorphic paradigm, commonplace in profane anthropology, is much less a part of theological discourse, probably due to its pagan roots. However, the concept of transformation was highly relevant during this period, in which debates over free will and predestination were frequent. As we have seen, the humanists considered Proteus a symbol of the freedom to forge one's own destiny, to be open to all aspects of the real; and this mutability was the more exalted as it made possible an ascending impulse that allowed man to follow a moral or spiritual path leading to self-transcendence. This was the meaning of Vivès's fable: by making judicious use of his freedom, man could share the feast of the gods. This latitude accorded to created being is not wholly alien to a certain theological approach emphasizing man's ability to earn his salvation. For example, Catholic thinkers of the Counter-Reformation, especially those under Jesuit influence, asserted that sin could be atoned for by action and the power of the will. Theologians of this stripe, sharing the optimism of the humanists, would probably not have disapproved of the philosophy of freedom incarnated by Proteus.

By contrast, the Protestant thinkers looked upon the myth of metamorphosis as questionable on several fronts. Beyond its roots in the ancient and polytheistic tradition, its affinity with the doctrine of free will made it immediately suspect; its ties with animistic, pantheistic, and even magical ways of thinking only reinforced this condemnation.

It is interesting to note that Pierre Viret, one of the mainstays of Calvinist Reform, devoted an entire treatise, *Metamorphose chrestienne*,[47] to this subject, thereby confirming the vogue and effectiveness of this model even among those hostile to it. It is of course true that the good pastor does not pass up an opportunity to express the repugnance he feels about the pagan connotations of his subject. Quoting Pythagoras, Ovid, and Apuleus, he refers to their fables of transformation and transmigration only in order to use them *ad maiorem gloriam Dei* and for the edification of the faithful:

> I wanted to write of Metamorphoses of another kind, metamorphoses consistent with Holy Scripture in which there is neither fable nor fiction. The Word of God has its own Metamorphoses, but they are of a rather different order than those of dreamy Philosophers and prevaricating Poets.[48]

If the humanists sing the praises of Proteus, Viret presents a totally different and opposed view: Proteus, he says, is the very image "of the inconstancy and violence of human affections."[49] Rethinking the concept of metamorphosis within a Christian perspective, he will make it the cornerstone of a Protestant anthropology.

In its Calvinist version, metamorphosis is emblematic of the Fall. Man, who was perfect when God created him, was transformed by sin: "I am speaking of a form of Metamorphosis that lies in the changing of hearts, understanding, and morals of corrupt and perverted men."[50] The angel was transformed into a beast. Subjugated by nature and reason, deprived of grace, man in fact leads an animal existence: "Because man isolated himself from God, without Whom he can have no Good ... in regard to his body and its affections, he is transformed into a brute beast, and in regard to the soul and the spirit, he is transformed into a devil."[51] Dog, snake, wolf, fox: man has become all of them. For example, says Viret, take a look at the warrior, armed with weapons, decked out in armor: he has the look and bearing of an animal, he seems covered with scales. Herein lies the real meaning of metamorphosis: man transformed to beast embodies the degradation of the sinner and the misery of life without God.[52]

The pagan poets were thus correct: although unintentionally, they provided us with an accurate picture of the human condition. On this point in agreement with the humanists, Viret is prepared to credit the pagan poets with having participated indirectly in the Revelation: "They had some obscure understanding of it."[53] Interpreted allegorically, these narratives of metamorphosis tell the truth about man. But at the same time these same pagan poets are wrong; they are wrong because they took these fables literally and presented them as such. They tried to convince us that a person could really turn into a stag, ox, or wolf. Such fictions nourish the worst kind of superstitions and are in obvious contradiction with the teachings of the Bible. How could a human being, endowed with a soul and whom God created in his own image, truly become an animal? How could the various species, whom God created separately and once and for all, change into each other? The real scandal of these metamorphoses is that they overthrow the order of Creation. Viret insists that fallen man was changed qualitatively, not substantively: the mutation was not of a physical but a moral order.

Although metamorphosis is thus an ambivalent symbol, it does have the merit of illustrating, in two distinct ways, the nature of human existence. While it indicates the depravity of the created being, it can also symbolize the process of redemption. On the one hand, the fall into sin; on the other, salvation by Grace. God allowed us to be deformed, but he can also reform us: we are in his hands just as "the earthen vessel is in the potter's hands: he can make, unmake, and remake it; form, deform, and reform it; break, smash, and repair it."[54]

The distance separating Pico della Mirandola, with whom this essay began, from Pierre Viret, with whom we close, is as great as that between Catholicism and Protestantism, freedom and predestination: man, from the point of view of the Florentine humanist, is master of his own destiny; from the point of view of the Swiss Protestant he is subject to the will of God. Renaissance anthropology is contained within these two boundaries. Although the gap between them is vast, they share a similar sensitivity to the transformations of created life and the flux of existence.

Notes

1. The *Oratio de hominis dignitate* serves as a preliminary discourse to the disputation (that did not take place) of the nine hundred theses, published in Rome in 1486, which Pic wanted to debate with other philosophers. The *oratio* appeared for the first time in a posthumous edition of the *Oeuvres complètes*. I am using here the translation by Yves Hersant, *De la dignité de l'homme*, Paris, 1993.
2. Ibid., p. 7.
3. Ibid., p. 7f.
4. Ibid., p. 13.
5. Ibid., p. 9.
6. *Fabula de homine* (1518), in: *Opera omnia*, 8 vols., Valencia, 1782-1790, Vol. 4, pp. 1-8. Engl. transl. in: E. Cassirer, P. Kristeller, and J.H. Randall Jr. (eds.), *The Renaissance Philosophy of Man*, Chicago, 1948, pp. 387-93.

7. M. Ficin, *Théologie platonicienne* (1482), Vol. 14, 3: "Sixième signe. L'âme tend à devenir toutes choses." I am quoting here from the translation by R. Macrel, *Théologie platonicienne. De l'immortalité des âmes*, 3 vols., Paris, 1964, Vol. 2, pp. 256-59.
8. Ibid., p. 257.
9. Ibid.
10. Ibid., p. 258.
11. Ibid.
12. Ibid., pp. 256f.
13. Montaigne *Essais*, Vol. 1, 3 (ed. by P. Villey), Paris, 1965, p. 15: "Nous ne sommes jamais chez nous, nous sommes toujours au-delà."
14. On Petrarch's movements see N. Mann, *Petrarch*, Oxford, 1984; see also T. M. Greene, "The Flexibility of the Self in Renaissance Literature," in: P. Demetz et al. (eds.), *The Disciplines of Criticism: Essays in Literary Theory. Interpretations and History*, New Haven, 1968, pp. 241-64.
15. Term by D. Letocha, "Preface," in: idem, *Aequitas, Aequalitas, Auctoritas. Raison théorique et légitimation de l'autorité dans le XVe siècle européen*, Paris, 1992, p. xii. See also the excellent article by D. Russell, "Conception of Self and the Generic Convention. An Example from the *Heptameron*," in: *Sociocriticism*, 4-5 (1986-87), pp. 159-83; T.M. Greene (note 14 above).
16. Letter 854 (19 July 1518) in: A. Gerlo and P. Foriers (eds.), *Erasme. Correspondance*, 11 vols., Brussels, 1967, Vol. 3, p. 380, also for the following.
17. Letter 868 (Erasmus to Ambroise Leo, Louvain, 15 October 1518), in: ibid., p. 434.
18. Letter to Jean Botzheim, Basle, 30 January 1523, in: ibid., Vol. 1, p. 2.
19. Ibid., pp. 36-9.
20. See the comments on *Herculei labores* in: *Adages*.
21. L. Febvre, "Preface," in: J. Huizinga, *Erasme*, Paris, 1955, p. 8. Huizinga's biography illustrates Erasmus's versatility.
22. To Erasmus's diatribe (*De libero arbitrio*, 1524), Luther responded with his *De servo arbitrio*.
23. Quoted in T.M. Greene (note 14 above), p. 249. In this piece one finds some very good pages on the sixteenth-century popularity of treatises on education.
24. See, for example, *De copia. Ratio studiorum. De civitate morum puerilium, Colloquia*.
25. Vergerius quoted in: T.M. Greene (note 14 above), p. 249: "*Dum faciles animi iuvenum, dum mobilis aetas.*"
26. H. Chamard (ed.), *La Deffence et Illustration de la Langue françoyse*, Vol. 1, 3, Paris, 1961, p. 27. See also Du Bellay, "Ample discours au Roy (...)," in: H. Chamard (ed.), *Oeuvres poétiques*, 6 vols., Paris, 1908-31, Vol. 6, p. 233.
27. *Essais* (note 13 above), Vol. 2, 17.
28. See Machiavelli's *Prince*, Castiglione's *Le Courtisan*, Della Casa's *Galateo*, and Guazzo's *La Civil Conversazion*, as well as numerous rhetoric treatises.
29. See, for example, Erasmus's *Enchiridion Militis christiani* and Calvin's *Institution de la Religion chrétienne*.
30. Rabelais, *Gargantua*, Ch. 14; M. Huchon (ed.), *Oeuvres complètes*, Paris, 1994, p. 43.
31. Ibid., Ch. 23, p. 65.

32. Ibid., p. 64.
33. Important comments on this in D. Russell's article (note 15 above).
34. I have tried to explain this phenomenon in "Le récit modulaire et la crise de l'interprétation. A propos de l'*Heptaméron*," in: *Le Défi des signes. Rabelais et la crise de l'interprétation à la Renaissance*, Orléans, 1994, pp. 53-74.
35. *Essai* (note 13 above), Vol. 1, 26, p. 152.
36. Ibid., p. 167.
37. Ibid., Vol. 3, 2, p. 804.
38. Ibid., Vol. 2, 37, p. 784.
39. Ibid., Vol. 3, 2, p. 804.
40. Ibid., p. 811.
41. Ibid., pp. 807, 811, 813, respectively.
42. See A. B. Giamatti, "Proteus Unbound: Some Versions of the Sea God in the Renaissance," in: P. Demetz et al. (eds.) (note 14 above), pp. 437-75.
43. I have used here N. Comes, *Mythologie, ou Explication des Fables (...)*, Paris, 1627, p. 870.
44. Ibid.
45. V. Cartari, *Le Imagini dei Dei de gli Antichi*, Venice, 1571, p. 257.
46. Ronsard, *Continuation des Amours*, Vol. 1, 5, in: P. Laumonier (ed.), *Oeuvres complètes*, 20 vols., Paris, 1914-1975, Vol. 7, pp. 121f.
47. *Metamorphose chrestienne, faite par dialogue*, Geneva, 1561. The summary of the first part, given on the title page, points straight away to the importance accorded to the mobility of forms: "1. L'homme naturel; 2. L'homme difformé; 3. La transformation des ames; 4. Le vray Homme, ou l'Homme reformé." Another treatise by Pierre Viret (*Dialogues du desordre qui est a present au monde*, Geneva, 1545) is an early version of *Metamorphose*.
48. *Metamorphose* ("Advertissement"), f. Aiiv.
49. *Dialogues*, p. 733.
50. *Metamorphose* ("Advertissement"), f. Aiiv.
51. *Metamorphose*, pp. 113f.
52. Frank Lestringant in his Preface to his edition of Agrippa d'Aubigne's *Les Tragiques* (Paris, 1995, p. 10) refers to the same phenomenon: "*Les Tragiques* sont ainsi remplis de bien étranges métamorphoses: tyrans 'allouvis,' qui quittent la table pour se ruer sur les humains à la manière de loups-garous, juges transformés en fauves parqués dans des tanières et ayant de la chair humaine entre les dents, roi travesti en courtisane, à perruque et vertugadin, courtisans en chiens et en singes, le Louvre en ménagerie, le Palais de Justice en Enfer, les églises en lupanars ou en cabinets d'aisance."
53. *Metamorphose*, p. 114.
54. Ibid., p. 110.

Shaped in the Image of Reason
The World According to Sherlock

Gerhard van der Linde

The detective fiction of the tradition initiated by Poe and Conan Doyle and continued by Agatha Christie, Dorothy Sayers, Rex Stout and others proposes the unquestioning acceptance of cognitive rationality[1] as a virtually infallible tool for problem solving and as an instrument of knowledge.[2] In the Holmes narratives, linear reasoning, based on observation grounded in the assumption that phenomena can be "read" in terms of a direct correlation between visual detail and connotative or denotative meanings, is presented as the only true path towards knowledge and understanding. Thus, the narratives implicitly discard the critical and autonomous rationality proposed by Kant.[3] Through their dogmatic insistence on a particular analytical method, they advocate a monist rationality which is repressive and alienated from the reader, in that s/he is not required to be a critical participant, but remains a passive admiring onlooker.

The 56 short stories which Conan Doyle wrote about Holmes all follow the same basic pattern: the problem to be solved is explained to the detective, usually by a client. Holmes frequently asserts his authority in the initial sequences by drawing inferences concerning either the narrator or the client, or both, which illustrate his intellectual superiority. In the course of the investigation, he identifies vital clues and constructs hypotheses concerning the solution of the problem. The other characters are almost always unable to follow his reasoning or draw the correct inferences from the data presented to them. Once the criminal has been identified, he is confronted, or Holmes explains his reasoning to an admiring audience, or both. The consistent adherence to a basic pattern in the Holmes narratives demonstrates the conventionality of traditional detective fiction. Conan Doyle's successors even proposed a codification of the subgenre,[4] which can be viewed as the extreme manifestation of an element found in all traditional detective fiction, namely, the desire to project an orderly, consistent reality through a closed, self-sufficient text.

The reader of traditional detective fiction is the passive recipient of a fictional world of which the coherence and consistence are pre-determined by literary conventions. In the Holmes narratives and elsewhere, he is merely an admiring spectator to the detective's accomplishments. This confirms Sciascia's observation that,

> il medio lettore di polizieschi, e cioè il miglior lettore di questo genere narrativo, è, insomma, colui che non si pone come antagonista dell'investigatore a risolvere in anticipo il problema, a 'indovinare' la soluzione, a indovinare il colpevole: il buon lettore sa che la soluzione c'è già, alle ultimissime pagine ... e che il divertimento, il passatempo, consiste nella condizione – di assoluto riposo intellettuale – di affidarsi all'investigatore ....[5]

The detective's unassailably superior position is often entrenched though exclusion and repression:

> Nei romanzi del genere sono impiegati senza precauzione – senza la precauzione, cioè, che è dell'arte – dei mezzi che con notevole approssimazione si possono definire di terrore: e l'effetto è fuga di pensieri. Meditazione senza distacco.[6]

Accordingly, the weaknesses and mistakes of Holmes's rivals are highlighted and their theories even ridiculed. The official police is usually presented as rather stupid and unimaginative, sometimes as guilty of smugness and careless thinking. Thus, for example, Athelney Jones, in *The Sign of Four*, premises his investigation by asserting: "Stern facts here – no room for theories."[7] He "realistically" assumes that "facts" are equivalent to what is immediately evident, yet his observations do not seem to be very accurate. Several important clues have to be pointed out to him by Holmes. Jones constructs a hypothesis before he has all the relevant data at his disposal, which is not necessarily inadmissible, provided that it is treated as a tentative hypothesis, to be tested and modified as required.[8] Jones, however, obtusely refuses to modify this initial hypothesis; he obstinately sticks to it, without being put off by data, brought to his attention by Holmes, which contradict it. Instead, he tries to make the data fit his theory. He mistakenly wants to use a hypothesis to explain data not taken into account in its construction, and which it is not powerful enough to explain. His conclusions are based on a series of propositions, each of which, taken separately, seems plausible, but between which no compelling connection is being established. Therefore, the conclusions cannot be accepted.

The secondary characters inaccurate reasoning is further illustrated in *A Study in Scarlet*. Having found the letters "RACHE" "scrawled in blood-red letters" at the scene of the crime, the official detective, Lestrade infers that the criminal "was going to put the female name Rachel, but was disturbed before he or she had time to finish."[9] Holmes, of course, knows that the letters form the German word for "revenge." There are several reasons for Lestrade's error. Firstly, his frame of reference is too limited: he does not know any German. A second weakness is that Lestrade's inference is inconclusive and overcomplicated. Its accuracy cannot be established before further data have been collected, as it rests on a new hypothesis (the criminal was "disturbed"), which would have to be corroborated in turn. By contrast, Holmes's explanation is simple and self-sufficient. It contains fewer premises than Lestrade's and does not introduce new elements to the case. In terms of simplicity it is therefore superior.[10] It is also more powerful in that, apart from explaining the letters, it suggests a motive for the crime.[11] Lestrade's inferences are not wholly implausible, yet the narrative presents them as obviously false, thereby affirming Holmes's superiority.

Watson, the narrator acts as a foil for Holmes's intellectual giftedness. He states in one of the later stories that his "methodical slowness" might have irritated the detective, but that it "served only to make his own flame-like intuitions and impressions flash up the more vividly and swiftly."[12] Watson's being intellectually less gifted than his friend is one of the fixed points of these narratives. Time and again, confronted by the same data as Holmes, he fails to draw the correct inferences. In some cases, this is due to his not possessing the relevant knowledge. For example, in *A Scandal in Bohemia*, he guesses that the letters woven into the paper of the letter received from Holmes's client indicate the "name of the maker." Holmes, with his superior reservoir of factual knowledge, refutes this and provides the correct explanation. In other cases, Watson simply fails to draw any inferences whatsoever from the data he observes. He is unable to achieve the scientist's goal of finding "an explanation from the data."[13] A further problem is that he tends to ignore particulars he regards as marginal, thereby overlooking important clues, while Holmes repeatedly insists that even the most trivial detail might be vital to the investigation.

Holmes's superiority in itself does not explain his rivals' consistent incompetence. It seems implausible that both detectives from the prestigious Scotland Yard and a medical doctor – a trained scientist – would be consistently unable to solve any of the crimes narrated, or at least to draw a certain number of accurate inferences. The dual aim of such distortion is to confirm Holmes's unassailable status as supreme detective, and the repression of a dialogical search for truth. This results in the valorization of a monolithic rationalism.

No alternatives are allowed to the type of rationality propagated by Holmes. His arch enemy, Moriarty, his only equal amongst criminals, is in effect a mirror image of himself: pure intellect, but devoted to evil, not to the furtherance of justice. Holmes's brother, Mycroft, his only other equal amongst the secondary characters, is described in terms which call to mind a contemporary database:

> We will suppose that a Minister needs information as to a point which involves the Navy, India, Canada, and the bimetallic question, he could get his separate advices from various departments upon each, but only Mycroft can focus them all, and say offhand how each factor would affect the other ... In that great brain of his everything is pigeonholed, and can be handed out in an instant.[14]

Thus, the Holmes narratives present rationality exclusively as a tool for problem solving; implicitly define reason only in terms of cognitive rationality.[15] The Enlightenment idea of reason as a vehicle for emancipation[16] is not here at play. The knowledge attained by the detective does not enlighten, but confirms the privileged status of a particular type of rationality.

A characteristic of Holmes's approach is his detachment from the object of his investigation, viewed as a precondition for the emergence of truth. Towards the beginning of *A Scandal in Bohemia*, for example, Watson states: "All emotions ... were abhorrent to his cold, precise, but admirably balanced mind."[17] Further on, he continues:

> He never spoke of the softer passions, save with a gibe and a sneer. They were admirable things for the observer ... But for the trained reasoner to admit such intrusions into his own delicate and finely adjusted temperament was to introduce a distracting factor which might throw a doubt upon all his mental results.[18]

Holmes's own view is that, "detection is, or ought to be, an exact science, and should be treated in the same cold and unemotional manner."[19] He takes a completely impersonal view of his clients; each should be seen as 'a mere unit, a factor in a problem.'"[20] Objectivity, the scission between the knowing subject and the objects of knowledge, underpins the deterministic world view implicit in the traditional detective novel, that is, the assumption that phenomena can be explained clearly and with certainty in terms of cause and effect, of fixed laws and a stable, well-defined order.[21] It is a basic assumption of classical deterministic theories that objective reality is stable and wholly independent of the observer; it is an assumption refuted, *inter alia*, by the findings of quantum theory, which showed that the object of investigation can change according to the experimental setup and the observer's point of view.[22]

Thus, determinism by implication divides the rational subject into diametrically opposite and completely separate halves: on the one hand, detachment, objective rationality and precision; on the other, the emotions and the instincts. The passions are viewed as superfluous and irrelevant to objective knowledge; as belonging to the "lower realm." Like certain biological processes, they are relegated to the secret, unmentionable corners of the rationalist subject's existence. In terms of classical rationalism, "Ciò che èmeramente fisico, materiale o semplicemente individuale o specifico, costituisce la bassa empiria."[23] Classical rationalism introduces a hierarchical division between mind and body, between rationality, on the one hand, and the emotions and instincts, on the other.

Accordingly, in the Holmes narratives,

> i riferimenti a ciò che è corporeo, all'orina, agli escrementi, alla fame, ai cattivi odori, e simili rappresentano da un lato una sconvenienza e dall'altro qualcosa di irrelevante ... rappresentano ciò che è degradante, volgare nella vita degli uomini ... nulla offrono che possa contribuire alla comprensione di alcunchè pertanto sono destinati a cadere al di fuori della stessa razionalità.[24]

Indeed, Conan Doyle deals with crime without dwelling on its more disconcerting aspects. Virtually no information is supplied on the unsavory aspects of Victorian society. Even though their presence is a *sine qua non*, the criminals in these narratives remain mere pretexts. Conan Doyle's vision of society in the Holmes narratives is rather prudish and naive; crimes and criminals are viewed at a distance and appreciated for their entertainment potential.

Holmes's asexuality and misogyny tie in with this. He is not in the least influenced by the sexual, and is completely immune to the potentially disruptive charms of the feminine. Female sexuality and seduction are absent from the Holmes narratives. To some extent, this can be attributed to the prudishness of the Victorian era, but a more important motivation is the assumption that cognitive rationality should be safeguarded against the passions. The institutional and the feminine are repressed because they might theaten the harmonious wholeness of reason, which postulates clinical "objectivity," assumed to render the world transparently accessible to knowledge and understanding, as a precondition and guarantee for truthfulness.

Grounded in reason, Holmes's observations are presented as invariably accurate, thus demonstrating the certainty presumably achieved only through scientificity. The reader is confronted with a supposedly scientific, that is, clinically objective method of detection, which constitutes a closed, self-sufficient system, immune to doubt. The status of Holmes's method is such that his theories are not viewed as mere statements about the world, but as reality itself; there is no distance between the theories and the objective world, but harmonious coincidence.[25] In the Holmes narratives, no explicit distinction is made between the detective's conjectures and statements of fact. Holmes's inferences are assumed to correspond to the "true" state of affairs, to give direct access to knowledge or reality itself. Contrary to Popper,[26] Holmes presents correspondence to the facts, or objective truth as quite attainable.

Accordingly, the narrator's admiration for Holmes is wholly unconditional, almost servile: "Sufficient for me to share the sport and lend my humble help without distracting that intent brain with needless interruption."[27] Holmes's inferences are often "framed" by expressions of astonished admiration.[28] Watson and the other secondary characters' inability to follow his reasoning provide him with opportunities to set out his theories. The few instances of skepticism on the part of his audience do not call into question the validity of Holmes's methods or the accuracy of his findings, but merely provide further opportunities for him to demonstrate his intellectual superiority and confirm the incontrovertibility of his conclusions. [29]

The authority of Holmes's inferences is grounded in premises which are never subjected to serious questioning. It also derives from the attributes of the detective himself: he is presented as being of superior, even superlative intellect: "The most perfect reasoning and observing machine;"[30] "extreme exactness and astuteness."[31] Holmes himself refers to "work" (that is, his processes of reasoning) "of the utmost finesse and delicacy."[32]

Frequently, an illustration *of* his abilities is provided in the early stages of a case. In *The Red-headed League*, for example, the narrator endeavors "after the fashion of my companion to read the indications which might be presented by" their client's "dress or appearance."[33] He concludes that the man can only be described as average, commonplace; that there is "nothing remarkable" about him "save his blazing red head, and the expression of extreme chagrin and discontent upon his features." Watson simply gives a description of external particulars.

The detective introduces his inferences in this story with a litotes, thus diminishing the difficulty of the problem "beyond the obvious facts ...."[34] According to Perelman,[35] the litotes can be defined "as a manner of expression which seems to weaken the thought." By describing the facts as "obvious," Holmes downplays his own abilities, and thus, highlights the discrepancy between his perspicacity and his rivals' lack of insight. He ironically suggests that one can assume the "facts" to be *obvious* to all the members of his audience; the incompatibility of such an assumption with the actual situation casts ridicule upon his rivals.[36]

Holmes's inferences in this story are based on abductive reasoning (big right hand – manual labour; shiny right cuff – "considerable amount of writing"), that is, conjecture indicating a possibility which can be calculated in terms of probability;[37] connotation ("arc and compass breastpin" – Freemasonry); and specialized factual knowledge (which enables him to establish the Chinese origin of the tattoo mark on his client's wrist).

The client's initial reaction to these inferences is one of astonishment. Once Holmes's reasoning has been explained to him, however, he responds with a litotes: "... I see there was nothing in it after all."[38] The client seems to be unaware that this remark reflects ironically on his own abilities: if there was "nothing in it" in the first place, then why was he so slow to understand?

Holmes's ironical reference to his "poor little reputation, such as it is,"[39] obliquely ridicules the obtuseness of his audience: it indicates an attitude of mock humility, an ironical overestimation of his audience's abilities. The whole passage in question is built upon binary oppositions, such as secondary vs. primary levels of signifiers, or implied vs. evident meanings; intelligence vs. obtuseness; penetration vs. lack of penetration. The first element in each pair is linked to Holmes, which affirms the superior vs. inferior relationship between him and the secondary characters.

The official policeman in this narrative, Athelney Jones, belittles Holmes, firstly, by implying that he is only capable of "starting a chase," and secondly, by insinuating that he is inexperienced.[40] The reader knows both suggestions to be untrue, which discredits Jones. In addition, he uses the metaphor "an old dog" in order to claim for himself the authority of extensive experience. A reader who made his acquaintance in *The Sign of Four*, however, would be aware of Jones's lack of success. The metaphor could therefore also be understood to mean: "Rich in experience of failure." It acquires ironical overtones which make Jones appear ridiculous.

Jones describes Holmes's methods as "just a little too theoretical and fantastic." In fact, as the reader knows, Holmes repeatedly cautions against theorizing on the basis of insufficient data; his own inferences are based on observation and empirical knowledge. Moreover, in *The Sign of Four*, Jones provides ample evidence of his own tendency towards drawing hasty inferences or constructing a hypothesis and then trying to adapt the data to it, instead of the other way round, like Holmes. Jones finds the superdetective's conjectures "fantastic" because he himself believes, in agreement with the commonsense theory of knowledge, that truth is self-evident and directly accessible through observation.⁴¹ Yet even in terms of this approach, Jones fails as his observations are often inaccurate.

In an attempt to belittle Holmes, Jones inadvertently uses litotes and euphemism, but merely succeeds in weakening his position:

> You may place confidence in Mr. Holmes, sir ... He has his own little methods, which are, if he won't mind my saying so, just a little too theoretical and fantastic, but he has the makings of a detective in him. It is not too much to say that once or twice ... he has been more nearly correct than the official force.⁴²

Throughout this section, Jones is made to look ridiculous by the discrepancy between his statements and the reader's knowledge about his achievements as compared to Holmes's. The contrast is presented in an obvious and unequivocal, perhaps even crude manner. As a result, Jones's inferiority to Holmes almost seems exaggerated.

Sometimes, Holmes's authority is emphasized by the secondary characters' silence. In *The Adventure of the Naval Treaty*, for example, the detective's assertion that the letter received by the narrator was written by a woman is not questioned; although Holmes does not present any evidence for the statement, it is tacitly accepted as accurate. The lack of evidence is not mentioned, which reaffirms the narrator's almost servile acquiescence to Holmes's reasoning.

Elsewhere, the detective interrupts the client's narrative of the problem to indicate that an important clue has been identified. "That is of enormous importance," said Holmes.⁴³ No further explanation is forthcoming, though the client evidently does not understand why that particular aspect of his narrative should be viewed as significant. This again indicates that Holmes's abilities are beyond the comprehension of the other characters, and highlights the exclusiveness of his position as the "one who knows." He usually explains his reasoning, but the explanation is often deferred in order to confirm his power and authority.⁴⁴

The Adventure of the Naval Treaty again offers a stark contrast between Holmes and the representative of the official police, who states categorically: "There was absolutely no clue of any kind;"⁴⁵ Holmes identifies seven clues.⁴⁶ Further on, he tells his client: "The principal difficulty in your case ... lay in the fact of there being too much evidence."[47] Here, the relationship between Holmes and the official police again has the nature of a binary opposition between insight and the lack thereof. Holmes's status as the Master, as the "one who knows" is evident. It is consistent with this that he should explain his reasoning in a "didactic fashion."[48]

The binary opposition initiated/uninitiated is also implicit in the relationship between Holmes and his clients. Thus, mystified by his inferences, James M Dodd, in *The Adventure of the Blanched Soldier*, describes him as a "wizard," and states hyperbolically: "You see everything."[49] To the uninitiated Dodd, Holmes's reasoning seems an almost impenetrable mystery. The rigid line of demarcation between initiated and uninitiated in the Holmes narratives constitutes the foundation for a rigid and unshakable power structure. The secondary characters (and, with them, the reader) can surrender themselves to the reassuring knowledge that order will be restored and transgression punished by a superior authority. shaped in the image of classical reason and governed by fixed, universal laws,[50] the world presented by the traditional detective novel always returns to equilibrium.

Despite his references to a "method," Holmes is not concerned with systematic theorizing or system-building. Without exception, the problems to be solved by him are of a practical nature. His task is not to uncover universal truths or ultimate meaning, but to find *ad hoc* explanations though a "reading" of the available data; to confirm the deterministic order of the world[51] through rational analysis. Accordingly, seemingly trivial particulars are shown to be meaningful, to fit into an overall pattern.

In the Holmes narratives, the intrusion of violence and disorder into the civilized *status quo* is neutralized through rational analysis and explanation. The potentially disruptive energy of sexuality is not allowed near the surface. It does not even feature prominently as a motive for crime; the true crime of passion is alien to Holmes's world. Even though the only real challenge to his authority is posed by a woman (Irene Adler, in *A Scandal in Bohemia);* she defeats him, not by exploiting her feminine charms, but simply by outwitting him. Thus, the supremacy of pure intellect remains unscathed.

Even the detective's drugtaking is presented as the counterpart to his mental exertions. It neither results from a biological urge, nor implies a search for physical sensations, but is merely a cure for mental *ennui*. The needs and functions of the body are never allowed to influence Holmes's actions and thought processes. Thus, his position is entrenched as the representative of a "pure" rationality, aimed at problem-solving, which operates within a strict mind-body dualism.

Notes

1. See H. Spinner, "Vereinzeln, verbinden, begründen, widerlegen: Zur philosophischen Stellung von Begründungs- und Kritikoptionen im Rahmen einer Systematik der Erkenntnisstile und Typologie der Rationalitätsformen," in: Forum für Philosophie (ed.), *Philosophie und Begründung*, Frankfurt, 1987, pp. 29f.
2. See U. Eisenzweig, *Le récit impossible: forme et sens du roman policier*, Paris, 1986, p. 14; Th. Narcejo, *Une machine à lire; le roman policier*, Paris, 1975, p. 239.
3. I. Kant, "Beantwortung der Frage: Was ist Aufklärung?" in: idem, *Schriften von 1783-1788*, Berlin, 1922, pp. 167-76.
4. See J. Symons, *Bloody Murder. From the Detective Story to the Crime Novel*, Harmondsworth, 1985, pp. 93-97.
5. L. Sciascia, *Cruciverba*, Turin, 1983, pp. 216f.
6. Ibid.
7. A. Conan Doyle, *The Sign of Four*, London, 1974, p. 37.
8. See K.R. Popper, *Objective Knowledge*, Oxford, 1979, pp. 258-60.
9. A. Conan Doyle, *A Study in Scarlet*, Harmondsworth, 1982, p. 33.
10. See G. Chaitin, "Randomness and Mathematical Proof," in: *Scientific American*, No. 232 (1975), p. 48.
11. See K.R. Popper, *Objective Knowledge* (note 8 above), p. 143.
12. A. Conan Doyle, *Sherlock Holmes. The Complete Short Stories*, London, 1985, p. 891.
13. N.R. Hanson, *Patterns of Discovery. An Inquiry into the Conceptual Foundations of Science*, Cambridge, 1961, p. 71.
14. A. Conan Doyle, *Sherlock Holmes* (note 12 above), p. 703.
15. See H. Spinner, "Vereinzeln" (note 1 above), p. 29.
16. See J.-F. Lyotard, *The Postmodern Condition. A Report on Knowledge*, Manchester, 1987, p. 31.
17. A. Conan Doyle, *Sherlock Holmes* (note 12 above), p. 3.
18. Ibid.
19. Idem, *The Sign of Four* (note 7 above), p. 15.
20. Ibid., p. 26.
21. See E. Morin, "I linguaggi della complessità," in: G. Barbieri and P. Vidali (eds.), *Le ragione possibile: per una geografia della cultura*, Milan, 1988, p. 420.

22. H. Pagels, *The Comic Code. Quantum Physics as the Language of Nature*, London, 1983, pp. 143-45.
23. A. Gargani, "Introduction," in: *Crisi della ragione*, Turin, 1979, p. 19.
24. Ibid., pp. 19f.
25. Ibid., pp. 9f.
26. K.R. Popper, *Conjectures and Refutations*, Oxford, 1989, p. 229.
27. A. Conan Doyle, *Sherlock Holmes* (note 12 above), p. 38.
28. Ibid., pp. 45, 58, 253, 260, 345f., 422, 470, 602ff.; Idem, *A Study in Scarlet* (note 9 above), p. 38.
29. See idem, *The Sign of Four* (note 7 above), pp. 18-20; see also W. Hüllen, "Semiotics Narrated: Umberto Eco's *The Name of the Rose*," in: *Semiotica*, Vol. 64, No. 1/2 (1987), p. 43.
30. A. Conan Doyle, *Sherlock Holmes* (note 12 above), p. 3.
31. Ibid., p. 36.
32. Ibid., p. 634.
33. Ibid., p. 24.
34. Ibid., p. 25
35. Ch. Perelman, *The New Rhetoric. A Treatise on Argumentation*, Notre Dame UP, 1971, p. 291.
36. Ibid., p. 292.
37. N. Harrowitz, "Il modello del detective: Charles S. Peirce e Edgar Allan Poe," in: U. Eco and Th. Sebeok (eds.), *Il segno dei tre: Holmes, Dupin, Peirce*, Milan, 1983, p. 220.
38. A. Conan Doyle, *Sherlock Holmes* (note 12 above), p. 25.
39. Ibid.
40. Ibid., p. 38.
41. See K.R. Popper, *Objective Knowledge* (note 8 above), p. 60.
42. A. Conan Doyle, *Sherlock Holmes* (note 12 above), p. 38.
43. Ibid., p. 394.
44. M. Truzzi, "Sherlock Holmes: psicologo sociale applicato," in: U. Eco and Th. Sebeok, *Il segno* (note 37 above), p. 76.
45. A. Conan Doyle, *Sherlock Holmes* (note 12 above), p. 396
46. Ibid., p. 399.
47. Ibid., p. 413.
48. Ibid.
49. Ibid., pp. 920f.
50. E. Morin, "I linguaggi" (note 21 above), p. 420.
51. Ibid.

Notes on the Contributors

Pascal Bouchery was born in 1960 and gained his doctorate in Anthropology from the University of Paris X in 1995. Associated with the Centre d'Anthropologie de la Chine du Sud et de la Peninsule Indochinoise, he has spent the last ten years researching the Tibeto-Burmese peoples of Thailand and South China.

Bénédictine Brac de la Perrière, born in 1958, is a researcher at CNRS's Laboratoire sur l'Asie du Sud-Est et le Monde Austronésien and a course director at the National Institute of Languages and Civilizations in Paris. Since 1981 she has regularly undertaken research trips to Burma and is interested in problems of urbanization in that country. Her other major research interest relates to the cult of possession in Burma and its pantheon on which she has published a book: *Les Rituels de possession en Birmanie. De culte d'Etat aux cérémonies privées*, 1989.

Laurence Caillet was born in 1947 and, following a research appointment at CNRS, is now professor of Ethnology at the University of Paris X. Since 1970 he has been involved in work on Japan and in particular on how the religious beliefs of the Japanese are being adapted to modern contexts. Among his publications: *Omizutori, le puisage de l'eau de jouvance*, 1981; *Fêtes et rites des quatre saisons au Japon*, 1981; *Le famille Yamasaki*, 1991.

Bernard Formoso was born in 1957. Having obtained his doctorate at the Ecole des Hautes Etudes en Sciens Sociales, he is currently lecturer in Ethnology at the University of Paris X. He is responsible for the "Asian Crossroads" project within the Laboratoire d'Ethnologie et de Sociologie Comparative (CNRS/Paris X). He has undertaken several research trips to Thailand, Laos, and South China since 1984. His special interest is in questions of religious synchretism in continental South-East China and of the identity of the Chinese living in Thailand. His most recent publiations in English: "Hsiu-Kou-Ku. The Ritual Refining of the Restless Ghosts among the Chinese of Thailand," in: *Journal of the Royal Anthropological Institute*, 2/1996; "The Chinese Philanthropic Associations in Thailand," in: *Journal of South-East Asian Studies*, 3/1996. There are also numerous publications of his in French.

Michel Jeanneret, born in 1940, is professor of French Literature and deputy dean of the Humanities Faculty of the University of Geneva. He has taught at Cambridge and has been visiting professor at Princeton, Harvard and Irvine. His publications include: *La Lettre perdue. Ecriture et folie dans l'oeuvre de Neval*, 1978; *Des Mets et des Mots. Banquets et propos de table à la Renaissance*, 1987; *Le Défi des signes. Rabelais e la crise de l'interpretation à la Renaissance*, 1994. His latest work is in press: *Perpetuum mobile. Métamorphose des corps et des oeuvres de Vinci à Montaigne.*

Gisèle Krauskopff was born in 1950 and is a researcher at CNRS's Laboratoire d'Ethnologie et de Sociologie Comparative. Since 1976 she has been to Nepal on numerous occasions where she has been studying the Tharu, and most recently the legitimation cults of Indo-Nepalese royalty. Publications: *Maîtres et Possédés. Les rites et l'ordre social chez les Tharu*, 1989; *Célébrer le pouvoir. Dasain, une fête royale au Népal*, edited with Marie Lecomte-Tilouine, 1996.

Marie Lecomte-Tilouine, born in 1962 and currently a researcher with CNRS. She received a doctorate from the Ecole des Hautes Etudes en Sciences Sociales in Paris. She is a member of the research project "Milieux, Sociétés et Cultures de Himalaya" and is a course director at the National Institute of Oriental Languages and Civilizations" in Paris.

She is a specialist on the Tibeto-Burmese Magar and has worked on Nepalese Hinduism and more generally on the transmission of symbolic forms in the Himalayan region. Publications: *Les Dieux du pouvoir. Les Magar et l'hinduisme au Népal entral*, 1993; *Célébrer le pouvoir. Dasain, une fête royale au Népal*, edited with Gisèle Krauskopff, 1996.

Gerhard van der Linde studied literature at the University of South Africa in Pretoria. He obtained his doctorate on cognitive rationality and indetermination in postmodern detective novels. He is currently working on investigative methods in the novels of Simenon and on the personality of Maigret. He has published numerous articles on postmodern literature.

Gábor Vargyas was born in Budapest in 1952 and is research director at the Institute of Ethnography in the Hungarian Academy of Sciences. He has taught ethnology at the University of Pest and of Eötvös Lorand (Budapest). He has undertaken numerous research trips to Neu Guinea and Vietman. In the latter country he studied religious ideas among the *brou*-speaking Austral-Asian peoples. Major publications: *Data on the Pictorial History of Northeast Papua-New Guinea*, 1986; *Field Notes from the Astrolabe Bay, Madang Province*, 1987; *Selected Bibliography of Hungarian Ethnology* (in collaboration with V. Kovacs and M. Sarkany), 1991.

IDENTITY, GENDER AND POVERTY IN RAJASTHAN
Experiences of a Tribalised Community

Maya Unnithan-Kumar, *Lecturer in Social Anthropology, School of African and Asian Studies, University of Sussex*

Most studies of the so-called tribal communities in India stress their social, economic, and political differences from communities that are organized on the basis of caste. It was this apparent contrast between tribal and caste lifestyle and, moreover, the paucity of material on tribal groups, that motivated the author to undertake this study of a poor "tribal" community, the Girasia, in northwestern India. While doing her fieldwork, she soon became aware that the traditional tribe-caste categories needed to be revised; in fact, she found them more often than not to be constructs by outsiders, mostly academic. Of greater importance for an understanding of the Girasia was the wider and more complex issue of self-perception and identification by others that must be seen in the context of their poverty as well as in the strategic and shifting use of kinship, gender and class relations in the region.

Contents: Introduction – Historical Background: the Rajput State and Related Identities – Rajputs and Girasias in Independent India: Identity Politics and Administration – Being a Girasia: the Lineage and the Village – Across Villages: Marriage Ideals, Practices and Strategies – Resource Management and the Divisions of Kinship and Gender – Girasia Brideprice and the Politics of Marriage Payments – Religion and the Experience of Kinship – Class, Resistance and Identity – Conclusions.

"... an extremely competent piece of ethnographic writing ... exceptionally well-written and organised." **Pat Caplan, Goldsmiths College**

October · ca. 224 pages · 1 map, 16 tables, 4 figs., 2 app., gloss., bibliog., index
ISBN 1-57181-918-5 · hardback

THE ARAKMBUT OF AMAZONIAN PERU
Andrew Gray

The Arakmbut are an indigenous people who live in the Madre de Dios region of the southeastern Peruvian rain forest. Since their first encounters with missionaries in the 1950s, they have shown resilience and a determination to affirm their identity in the face of many difficulties. During the last fifteen years, Arakmbut survival has been under threat from a gold rush that has attracted hundreds of colonists onto their territories. This trilogy of books traces the ways in which the Arakmbut overcome the dangers that surround them: their mythology and cultural strength; their social flexibility; and their capacity to incorporate non-indigenous concepts and activities into their defence strategies. Each area is punctuated by the constant presence of the invisible spirit, which provides a seamless theme connecting the books to each other.

Volume 1 MYTHOLOGY, SPIRITUALITY, AND HISTORY

Following the Arakmbuts' recommendation, the author uses their three greatest myths to introduce social, cultural and historical aspects of their lives. He ends with a discussion of the relationship between myth and history showing how the Arakmbut recreate their myths at the dramatic moments of their history.

'*...splendid and innovative ethnography...highly topical, well-written, intellectually highly interesting, and often avant-garde...sophisticated and honest discussions...*'
                              Joanna Overing, London School of Economics

June · ca. 272 pages · bibliog., 12 illus., index; ISBN 1-57181-876-6 · hardback

Volume 2 THE LAST SHAMAN   Change in an Amazonian Community

The death of a shaman in 1980 had enormous spiritual and political consequences for one of the Arakmbut communities, resulting in a shift in its social organization from comparative hierarchy to a more egalitarian system. The author uses this case as an illustration to challenge the idea that indigenous peoples live in fossilized, static worlds. He shows that political activities in conjunction with shamanic communication with the spirit world provide the impetus and context for change.

Winter · ca. 256 pages · bibliog., 12 illus., index; ISBN 1-57181-874-X · hardback

Volume 3 DETERMINING IDENTITY AND DEVELOPING RIGHTS

Over a period of about two decades the indigenous movement has grown into an international force, making a marked impact on the United Nations and the International Labor Organization. In this volume, the author looks at the growing consciousness among the Arakmbut who are increasingly demanding that their rights to their territories and resources should be respected in tandem with the growing development of indigenous rights internationally. However, the author points to a significant difference of perception: whereas non-indigenous human-rights legislation receives its legitimacy by judicial means, the Arakmbut find their legal system legitimized through the spirit world. The invisibility of this world makes it appear non-existent to non-indigenous observers. However, to overlook its importance prevents outsiders from understanding and appreciating its significance in the Arakmbut struggle for survival.

"*... a solid contribution to the understanding of the relationship between Amazonian notions and contemporary international legal concepts of human rights...(that) could become a reference text to be used in similar negotiations with other indigenous peoples.*"
                              L. E. Belaunde, University of Durham

March 1997 · ca. 288 pages 12 illus., bibliog., index; ISBN 1-57181-875-8 · hardback
ISBN 1-57181-886-3 · paperback

165 Taber Avenue • Providence, Rhode Island 02906
Phone: 401-861-9330 • Fax: 401-521-0046 • E-mail: BerghahnBk@aol.com

WARRIOR GENTLEMEN
'Gurkhas' in the Western Imagination

Lionel Caplan, *Professor of South Asian Anthropology, School of Oriental and African Studies, London*

Of late, there has been a growing interest in how non-Western peoples have been and continue to be depicted in the literatures of the West. In anthropology, attention has focussed on the range of literary devices employed in ethnographic texts to distance and exoticize the subjects of discourse, and ultimately contribute to their subordination. This study eschews the tendency to regard virtually all depictions of non-Western "others" as amenable to the same kinds of "orientalist" analysis, and argues that the portrayals found in such writings must be examined in their particular historical and political settings.

These themes are explored by analyzing the voluminous literature by military authors who have written and continue to write about the "Gurkhas", those legendary soldiers from Nepal who have served in Britain's Imperial and post-Imperial armies for more than two centuries. The author discovers that, instead of exoticizing them, the military writers find in their subjects the quintessential virtues of the European officers themselves: the Gurkhas appear as warriors and gentlemen. However, the author does not rest here: utilizing a wealth of literary, historical, ethnographic sources and the results of his own fieldwork, he investigates the wider social and cultural contexts in which the European chroniclers of the Gurkhas have been nurtured.

1995 · 192 pages · bibliog., index
ISBN 1-57181-852-9 · hardback

165 Taber Avenue • Providence, Rhode Island 02906
Phone: 401-861-9330 • Fax: 401-521-0046 • E-mail: BerghahnBk@aol.com

www.ingramcontent.com/pod-product-compliance
Lightning Source LLC
Chambersburg PA
CBHW071204070526
44584CB00019B/2915